"This book is a must-read for today's leaders and the leaders of tomorrow as it delivers a call to action around the true meaning and purpose of sustainable value creation . . . [and] provides a guideline and template for living a life of purpose."

—DAVID W. SCHNER,
president and executive editor,
LEADERS magazine

Charlie Moore never broke his stride after winning an Olympic gold medal in Helsinki in 1952. His professional life achievements feature notable accomplishments in business as well as successful leadership roles in college athletics, the arts, and, ultimately, in corporate philanthropy.

In *Running on Purpose* Moore has delivered a work that is not just a career memoir or an inspirational business book; it also champions family, resilience, persistence, the drive for results, strong communication, and other traits that can, and should, guide our personal and professional lives.

This is the remarkable first-person story of the action, tenacity, creativity, celebration, and principles that carried Moore from one success to another—and that ultimately led to his most important legacy: providing insights for guiding twenty-first-century American business.

More Advance Praise for
RUNNING ON PURPOSE

"Charlie Moore's winning an Olympic gold taught him that pursuing goals bigger than ourselves and striving for and committing to a bigger purpose give our lives meaning. His example of principled pursuit, his resilience and tenacity, and his positive attitude make his memoir fascinating, inspiring, and instructive."

—MARILYN CARLSON NELSON,
co-CEO, Carlson Holdings Inc.

"A constant theme Charlie has always championed is to give back, and *Running on Purpose* chronicles his spectacular journey. Many people, businesses, nonprofits, and our world are better off today because of Charlie's contributions."

—SANDY WEILL, former chair and CEO, Citigroup,
and the author of *The Real Deal*

"Charlie Moore knows better than most what it means to run on purpose. This book shares wisdom from Charlie's inspirational life and leaves readers with a clear impression of what it takes to be a strong leader."

—WILLIAM R. McDERMOTT, CEO, SAP SE,
and the author of *Winners Dream*

"Companies are recognizing that by leveraging their business capabilities and core competencies to improve society they can also achieve long-term financial benefits for their customers and shareholders. And Charlie has provided extraordinary leadership and vision, putting a spotlight on the importance and need to reimagine business's role in society. In *Running on Purpose* Charlie captures the spirit and essence of business and individual success through creating shared value. It's a must-read!"

—**TERRY McGRAW**, retired CEO, McGraw-Hill Companies

"Charlie is my refiring hero! His life is one of constant, tenacious, and inspirational movement. *Running on Purpose* is a lesson not just for individuals. The book also contains a powerful message for businesses to champion sustainable forms of growth. While Wall Street often suggests the only reason to be in business is to make money, I've always believed that profit is the applause you get for taking care of your customers, creating a motivating environment for your people, and being a good citizen in your community. We need to get CEOs to think in a different way."

—**KEN BLANCHARD**, author of *The One Minute Manager* and *Refire! Don't Retire*

"A new generation of investors is demanding financial performance and sustainability performance—as Charlie realized was inevitable and central to long-term resilience and value creation. Charlie's journey reminds us why 'carrying the torch' is more than just an Olympic expression. We must now accept the torch with honor and bring the same grace and courage to carrying it that Charlie has. Not because it is easy, but because it must be done for the benefit of companies, investors, and society."

—**JEAN ROGERS**, founder and CEO, Sustainability Accounting Standards Board

"When an Olympic gold medal winner and a company CEO writes a book about the need to change the game for how business is done, people should listen. I certainly have. Charlie is spot-on in his call for companies to focus on sustainable value creation and his challenge to companies and the individuals who work in them to 'dare to lead.' His writing style is like he is as a person— energetic, optimistic, wise, warm, and practical. This is a fun and important book to read!"

—**ROBERT G. ECCLES**, chairman, Arabesque Partners, and the author of *The Integrated Reporting Movement*

"As with everything in his life and career, Charlie infuses his memoir with empathy, intensity, and consistency. In calling for tenacity and creativity, he nudges businesspeople to stay outside of their comfort zones and highlights the extent to which building or rebuilding a business requires the open-minded embrace of change and transformation."

—**ERIKA KARP**, founder and CEO, Cornerstone Capital Group

"*Running on Purpose* captures the essence of Charlie Moore's rich personal journey. From winning Olympic gold to leading successful businesses and ultimately helping the world of corporate philanthropy become more effective, Charlie's story weaves an impressive tapestry of what it is possible to achieve and influence in one's life. His story provides a powerful road map for generations of future leaders to reach their fullest potential and lead business in the creation of sustainable value."

—**EDWARD B. RUST, JR.**, chairman of the board, State Farm Mutual Automobile Insurance

"Charlie Moore has inspired generations to succeed with purpose—from young Cornell athletes to the CEOs of Fortune 100 companies who embraced his leadership in driving the private sector toward higher societal values than simply making money. This book is about a principled lifetime of action that's always headed in the right direction."

—ROBERT S. HARRISON, chairman, board of trustees, Cornell University

"An inspired guide to the race the next generation of business leaders must run from a leader who has lived life with passion and purpose both on the track and in business."

—CHRIS PINNEY, president and CEO, High Meadows Institute

"This book is an important must-read for anyone who has the quality to lead rather than follow. The reflections are personal but for everyone. In the chapter The License to Lead, I am taken with the flow of the argument as well as the content. The call to action is not on one person or one institution, it is on everyone. Get your to-do list out. Charlie has laid out what we need to do and it is up to us to make it happen."

—PAUL DRUCKMAN, former CEO, International Integrated Reporting Council

"I have had the great fortune to observe and benefit from Charlie Moore's wisdom, broad perspective, and resilience in many phases of his career and life. What a gift it is that he is now teaching all of us the invaluable lessons he has learned from a remarkable life."

—DANIEL L. DOCTOROFF, founder and CEO, Sidewalk Labs

"Charlie Moore is a truly remarkable leader and community builder. The story of his multifaceted personal and professional journey should be read by anyone who cares about building better teams, better companies, better communities, and a better world. And by anyone who wants to gain insights into what it means to lead a meaningful and good life. He understands the importance of balancing financial success with social and environmental impact, and he sees the value in investing in the arts, education, and building resilient communities. *Running on Purpose* is without a doubt a must-read for both current and aspiring leaders from all walks of life."

—JANE NELSON, director, Corporate Social
Responsibility Initiative, Kennedy School of Government,
Harvard University

"*Running on Purpose* is the culmination of Charles Moore's diverse and dynamic life as a world-class athlete, innovator, change agent, business leader, and philanthropist. This book is a must-read for today's leaders and the leaders of tomorrow as it delivers a call to action around the true meaning and purpose of sustainable value creation. Charlie takes readers on his life journey, which is full of meaning, action, impact, and purpose. At a time when the world is full of challenges and turmoil, *Running on Purpose* provides a guideline and template for living a life of purpose."

—DAVID W. SCHNER, president and executive editor,
LEADERS magazine

"Wondering what the purpose of life is? This book is where you should begin to articulate your own purpose and sense of good in life. A smart and actionable book with an irrepressible and inspiring hero in Charlie."

—HENRIETTA H. FORE, chair and CEO,
Holsman International

"Charles Moore's life has been about top performance, critical problem solving, and delivering results and creating value for businesses, employees, and investors. Charlie exemplifies integrated thinking and now masterfully leverages that history into demonstrating how businesses and their leaders need to rethink how they report and communicate information on value creation. By advocating the use of integrated thinking and reporting, he makes the case for a new way of reasoning and communicating in the future."

—BARRY C. MELANCON, president and CEO,
American Institute of CPAs

"Charlie Moore's unbridled enthusiasm for leading a purpose-driven life is second to none. And at CECP, Charlie channeled that enthusiasm into building the largest and most impactful organization of its kind in history. This book beautifully captures the spirited zeal that Charlie has brought to his every endeavor. A very worthy read."

—DOUGLAS R. CONANT, retired CEO, Campbell Soup
Company, and author of *TouchPoints: Creating Powerful Leadership
Connections in the Smallest of Moments*

"Working closely with Charles Moore to develop an ambitious strategic plan and raise an audacious amount of money to support that plan was inspirational. His capacity to organize, communicate with, teach, and inspire volunteers and donors alike helped us easily exceed our goal. This book is another example of Charles's energy and purpose."

—DOUGLAS HALE, former head of school,
Mercersburg Academy

Praise for CHARLIE MOORE

"It is given to few by dint of their genes and hard work to win an Olympic gold medal. It is given to far fewer gold medalists to settle down from the distractions and blandishments of fame to create a successful career based on public service. Charlie Moore has achieved this in spades and I am proud to count him as my friend."

—SIR ROGER BANNISTER, author of *Twin Tracks* and *The Four-Minute Mile*

"Executive styles vary as widely as the companies they serve. Charlie Moore has been the consummate change agent in this respect. Heidrick & Struggles placed Charlie in four turnaround situations that demanded speed, discipline, and problem solving. In every appointment, a more lucid, resilient, and purposeful organization resulted. The decades we spent together became a true problem-solving partnership."

—GERARD R. ROCHE, chairman emeritus, Heidrick & Struggles

"Charlie Moore inspires the best of the human spirit. His personal achievements have only been exceeded by his pioneering leadership in social responsibility—setting the bar and inspiring excellence for all of us to follow."

—JAMES J. MURREN, chair and CEO, MGM Resorts International

RUNNING

on

PURPOSE

RUNNING
on
PURPOSE

Winning Olympic Gold,

Advancing Corporate Leadership,

and Creating Sustainable Value

CHARLES H. MOORE, JR.
with James Cockerille

Foreword by Richard Edelman

EDGEMOOR INK
2017

Visit www.runningonpurposebook.com

First published in 2017 by Edgemoor Ink.
Hardcover ISBN: 978-0-9983710-0-9
Paperback ISBN: 978-0-9983710-1-6
E-book ISBN: 978-0-9983710-2-3

Designed by Gregory Smith

Printed in the United States of America

In loving memory of Charles H. Moore, Sr., 1901–1983,

and Charles H. Moore III, 1951–2017

If you're going through hell, keep going.

—WINSTON CHURCHILL

CONTENTS

FOREWORD

The world is experiencing a crisis in confidence in institutions. Across the more than sixty countries surveyed for the Edelman Trust Barometer, trust in institutions among the general public is under 50 percent. By contrast, trust by informed elites is at the highest levels seen in the sixteen-year history of the annual study.

The most profound gap is in trust in business. In the United States, for example, 70 percent of elites trust business in contrast to only 51 percent of the general public. This antipathy plays out in a populist push against issues crucially important to business, such as free trade, genetically modified foods, and financial services regulation.

But despite skepticism about business's intent to do the right thing, the general public decidedly trusts business more than government. The gap in many countries we polled is more than 50 percent. Moreover, 80 percent of consumers believe businesses can both make money and improve society.

If business is looked to as a leader in solving society's ills, it is because of the path paved by people like Charlie Moore.

He is, in my view, a founding father of corporate social responsibility. Charlie's belief that business must take an active role in improving society is both a function of his intellect and bravery and also a testament to his patriotism. Without his foundational work, the leadership we see today from CEOs such as Apple's Tim Cook or Howard Schultz from Starbucks might not have come to be.

Charlie's ability to imagine what is possible comes from his hard work and humility. He was an Olympic gold medalist in the 400-meter hurdles in 1952, the CEO of three multinational manufacturing companies, the athletic director for Cornell University, and a member of the President's Council on Physical Fitness and Sports.

His story is inspiring—especially to the three men who tapped Moore to be executive director of the Committee Encouraging Corporate Philanthropy. In 1999, actor Paul Newman, former Goldman Sachs CEO John Whitehead, and real estate developer Peter Malkin formed CECP to address important societal challenges through the power of the private sector. When the three of them met Moore, Newman said, "Well, I guess we have to hire him. How many other CEOs have been gold medal winners?"

Moore brought unbelievable energy and passion to his job. I remember going with him to China, where he was to address one hundred Chinese companies on social responsibility. It was three in the afternoon, and the dreaded jet lag was kicking in for mere mortals like me. Moore was busy handing out his business card, asking the Chinese CEOs to come across for the next CECP conference, telling them about the upside of social responsibility for employee morale and community relations. He took personal responsibility for attracting new members, always starting at the top by asking board members to introduce him to CEOs. He would develop and cherish those relationships with the titans of industry, calling on Jeff Immelt of GE, Indra Nooyi of PepsiCo, and Klaus Kleinfeld of Alcoa, offering advice and spreading best practices. Upon retiring from CECP in 2013, Moore said his number one goal was to prove to Wall Street that there is a financial benefit to social responsibility—in brand reputation, employee loyalty, and risk mitigation.

The world's most successful companies today know that social purpose is an absolute must. The example set by Moore and the CECP elevated classic corporate philanthropy with a larger mandate that urged companies to fundamentally change their business practices to be smart and sustainable influences on society.

This is Moore's legacy and his greatest gift to the world.

—RICHARD EDELMAN,
President and CEO of Edelman

INTRODUCTION:
WHY THIS BOOK?

This book has been written for the individuals out there willing to sprint to the finish line. It's for those who search for real success in sometimes unorthodox ways. This book is for the principled person who wants to lead with vision, move among influential titans, and believes that traditional pathways must often be ignored in order to discover his or her truest potential.

I'M A SPRINTER AT HEART

This means chasing after everything I've ever chosen to focus on. It also means holding very little back and maintaining a lead throughout the run.

I've been characterized as driven, impatient, enthusiastic, critical, inspired, difficult, generous, demanding, larger-than-life, uncanny with the details, loving, competitive, smart, naïve—the list goes on as do the contradictions. But one thread remains that means the world to me. If Charlie Moore is involved, it's going to move quickly, be a lot of fun, and get done!

But don't get me wrong. I'm not averse to marathons. Many of the stories in this book are about substantially large undertakings. But I'll chop a long-distance run into smaller sprints any day.

And let's face it, life is a marathon. One I've been running for more than eighty-five years. Life is not a single undertaking with tightly related events but a series of exciting, swift *pursuits* full of truth and passion that culminate in a uniquely meaningful conclusion. With each string of purpose-fueled bursts comes a more deeply resilient frame of being.

But in this life, it was *action, tenacity, creativity,* and *principles* that carried me forward from one personal form of success to the next rather than my aiming for a distant, hard-to-see goal. How could I know what life would hold or where my abilities were best suited? Plus, there was always so much around me to celebrate.

The result has been a through line of action, joie de vivre, and resilience that anyone can rely on in their own life journey.

In writing this book, I want you to embrace a *pursuit mindset* for yourself and apply that urgency and purpose to building a better world. I want you to embrace big visions, take swift action, tame risk, pivot based on gut intuition, and overcome challenges along the way. And pass on what you feel and learn to others.

Let this story be a clue, therefore, not a prescription. Let it inform not only your legacy but also your confidence in the moment. Let it not drift into cold reflection but ignite a warm embrace and a push toward action!

Are you ready to get going?

Then get on your mark.

Get set.

Let's go!

RUNNING
on
PURPOSE

Chapter 1

THE RACE OF A LIFETIME

JULY 21, 1952: THE SUMMER GAMES OF THE XV OLYMPIAD

It was a Monday in Helsinki. A new moon.
I was twenty-two years old.

4:32 p.m.
Remove everything from your mind.

There I stood. Alone. Shrouded in a sea of pale crimson.

Beneath my cleats was a new oval of reddish crushed brick. Above me was a glowing mist as the track's reflection climbed up through the day's rain. Six carefully marked lanes traced and yawed their way into the distance. A divine hand, it seemed, had drawn solemn, jagged three-foot fences across them, cluttering the field's austere geometry.

There are no inanimate objects I've ever contemplated more.

3

Nothing matters but that first one.

The noise of 40,000 shifting spectators pumped and crackled through the wet atmosphere. Among them, my family. Dad. And I became vaguely aware of other bodies wearing numbers gathering nearby. Yuriy. John. Armando. Harry. Anatoliy. Stretching. Knotting laces. Warming up. I leaned down long enough to double knot my spikes.

Yuriy has never lost a race like this.

The race would be run in staggered lanes. Each athlete would run four hundred meters (or roughly a quarter-mile) over ten equally spaced three-foot-high hurdles. A racer running in an inside lane has a strong advantage because the field is mostly out ahead of him. In the outside lane, you cannot gauge your pace as there's not a single competitor in your view.

I had managed to draw inside lanes in all three of my earlier qualifying races. Now, in the most important race of my life, I had drawn the blind sixth lane running on the outside.

Twenty-two years old. Undefeated. Alone in an individual event.

We six finalists for the 400-meter hurdles removed our warm-up clothes, which were carefully placed in individual baskets and then transferred to the finish line. While my running shorts and shirt were plain white, I had a red, white, and blue stripe across my jersey that also displayed the USA Olympic crest and my competitor's number, 1006.

Each man pounded his starting blocks into place, a more sensible and secure method than the old process of digging holes in the cinder track with trowels.

4:43 p.m.
That first fence. Nothing else. For now.

My warm-up, mostly done in a tunnel under the stadium, was varied but not strenuous as I had run in the semifinals just two hours and forty minutes earlier. The rain, however, continued to vie for my attention, elbowing into my prerace ritual.

4:49 p.m.
Forget where you are. Forget home. Forget. Forget. Forget.

It was pouring by now. It had rained throughout the opening ceremonies and on the opening day of track competition when the first and second rounds of the 400-meter hurdles had been run. Ultimately, it would rain on seven of the eight days of Olympic track and field competition. The impact on speed was hard to calculate.

Forget the rain.

I had been sure to empty my bladder using the toilets set up under the stands in the stadium.

The time ticked toward five p.m. while the rain seemed to gently applaud the first track and field final of the Games of the XV Olympiad.

4:59:01 p.m.
What do I do? Get off with the gun and charge that first damned hurdle!

The starter, standing in lane six behind all the runners so he can see the entire field, barked, "On your mark," and the crowd grew quiet.

4:59:15 p.m.
Listen for it. Then move. Leap. Get out of your own way. Forget.

I had worked for this moment for seven jam-packed years.

When you are in "set" position, your mind does not wander. It shifts to another state. In this mental mode, economy of means prevails. It is a kind of meditative focus that empties the mind of everything but the moment and creates an acute instinctual awareness of every particular action needed in the race. This focus generates split-second responses that do not allow time for deliberation but rely on the instantaneous capture of the body below the surface of consciousness, which enables what has been practiced to become second nature.

4:59:55 p.m.
"Get set!"

The universe blinked and went oddly silent all around.

Bang! went the gun. And as if I had been struck by lightning, my thoughts went cold. Every leg, back, and neck muscle sprang with explosive force. I was determined to "pull the track" by staying ahead of the rest of the runners. I would reserve nothing even if it ripped me apart.

Over the first hurdle, the other runners had closed the starting gap. In the relative calm that this first leap afforded, my body's radar and prefrontal cortex came to a synaptic conviction: I was not in the lead. And I needed to be.

Speed was crucial. But so was stride since each hurdle reset my form. Take an even number of steps and you're forced to take the next hurdle with a different lead leg. Take shorter steps and you're going up and down more than forward. Sus-

Over the second hurdle but not in the lead yet.

taining an efficient pace between ten of those fences is the very art of the sport.

For this reason, I had pioneered a thirteen-stride approach and trained like hell to deliver it. This was an aggressive 13 percent decrease in the average fifteen-stride form.

But, remember, fourteen steps created a different set of problems. The nonstandard thirteen-step approach remains one of my proudest engineering accomplishments!

Taking advantage of my fewer steps between the second and third hurdles, I moved into the lead after the third hurdle. And despite my having run all-out in the semifinal earlier that day, I had reserves. Focus, form, and condition were synced. By the sixth hurdle, I had increased my lead to four yards. Over the seventh, I cut my stride back to take fifteen steps between the last three hurdles. But I was mad for the win, and despite fatigue setting in, I threw every muscle into clawing for more speed.

After the tenth hurdle, it was a sprint to the tape. And then it was done. A four-yard lead over Yuriy Lituyev of the Soviet Union.

The *United States 1952 Olympic Book* reports it this way:

> *He ran it as he always had—with a sprint start, a sprint middle and a finish manufactured of grit. Holland and Lituev [sic] were running with determination and courage and were challenging Moore all the way. Both appeared to come up on him in the home stretch but then Charlie threw his head up in the air, pumped his arms from hip to bobbing head, and galloped to the tape, ahead of the undefeated Russian by four yards when he crossed the line.*

The time on this spongy, rain-soaked raceway was 50.8 seconds. One-tenth of a second slower than the American record I held and tying the Olympic record I had set the day before in the second-round qualifiers.

I didn't best Glenn Hardin's world record of 50.6 set in 1934. But anyone who plays the horses can attest that tracks and weather conditions affect finishing times. Glenn won Olympic gold in Berlin with a time of 52.4 seconds, significantly slower than his best.

Tying my Olympic record in the 400-meter hurdles.

What if the track in Helsinki had been firmer? As the second athlete (after Glenn) to break 51 seconds, I have to wonder.

What would have been a much more thrilling test, however, would have been if Glenn and I had been able to race head-to-head!

Chapter 2

A PURSUIT MINDSET

The world is moving so fast these days that the one who says
it can't be done is generally interrupted by someone doing it.

—ELBERT HUBBARD

FROM THE WOODS

I can't remember a day I wasn't racing.

There are very few moments when I'm not prepping, attempting, completing, or instigating a rush to some goal or another. Many people would associate that with my hurdling and Olympic careers. But hurdles were simply another way to channel the rabbit in me.

Long before the track, it was the woods that taught my mind and body to move. Darting over the brush. Racing the sunset home. Hopping between footholds in a creek. Setting traps and swiftly exiting the scene. Even swinging from branches if it meant traversing a spot more effectively. I was a country boy, after all.

Later I would take horses and hounds overland in pursuit of foxes. Later still would come formal cross-country racing. But moving remained for me a form of play. Play with a sense of purpose.

The woods are not a simple place. They do not offer up patterns willingly. And well-worn paths disappear frequently under a fallen tree, harsh rainfall, or autumn's early leaves. This is part of a forest's allure for explorers. A gentle and constant reset of life's variables as if to say, "You better be paying attention!"

To find, memorize, and often create completely new trails was one of the earliest senses of vitality I can recall. The more I moved, the more I understood the land. The more I understood, the smarter my moves in the wild became. With such randomness underfoot, my body was engaged in all directions. And with an ecosystem of "toys" all around me, there was no end to the games I could create.

Those were solitary times for the most part. And any fun I had depended on the quality of the games I made up. But most children are naturally able to play make-believe with a minimum of inputs. But the scale, the complexity, the richness, and the openness of the woods engaged me in ways I still can't fully assess. I live in the woods now but still cannot fully grasp all of the mysteries and depths of that environment.

What I can say now, however, is that whenever I kept my goals as clear and fun and fluid as I had in those early days in the woods, I have succeeded. An example of this is perfecting my thirteen-step innovation that I can credit so many of my victories to and that is now standard in the 400-meter hurdles.

When I used this same routine for those I collaborated with, the experience was even more extraordinary. Whether I was in a boardroom, at the White House, on an Olympic medalist's rostrum, or at a family reunion, my world felt fullest when the path was kept to simple sprints. Though the bigger objective might be more of a marathon, the inspiration to act and the ability to maintain focus were one hundred times clearer when milestones were in sight.

It's my wish that this effort feels enthralling for everyone.

This inspired form of action is the sprinter's advantage—something I call the *pursuit mindset*, which is one part vision and one part action.

MEANINGFUL ACTION STARTS
WITH A VISION

Henry Ford once said that whether you think you can or you think you can't, you're right. And both outcomes matter. For good or bad, either outcome will influence a wide range of people. Your colleagues. Friends. Family. Yourself. That's how powerful your vision of success is.

Without revisiting the vast literature on productivity, personal development, or change management, I can tell you that most of what matters can be summarized as big visions but that advancing toward them relies on actual behaviors. For behavior to change, it becomes crucial to clarify the goals that are closer at hand, more specific in their fulfillment, or simply *easier* to understand.

As anyone who's familiar with SMART goals knows, it's easier to address each word in the acronym (specific, measurable, attainable, realistic, time-based) when defining a meeting than it is to determine the course of a new organization.

The difficulty is in the breadth of factors and the relative intangibility of outcomes. The more we focus our efforts on issues that are further from our present reality, the more open-ended and subjective things become. Timelines inevitably shift out, and for many big goals such as "prosperity" or "goodwill," an explicit end is not even desirable.

The pursuit mindset, therefore, craves the sprints to an accessible goal that simpler visions provide. The more of these you engage in, the more quickly you'll advance. The more facility you have in creating them for you and others, the more success you will enjoy.

Let's say you have a bigger objective in mind and want to shift your sights toward near-term sprints. I'm assuming the nature of it matters to you so I'm not making that an explicit criterion. Nonetheless, the quality of your pursuit's definition has a direct effect on your level of emotional involvement, energy, focus, and resilience.

Here are the hallmarks of successful pursuits:

The outcome is crystal clear in your mind. *Touching that tree on the other side of the field. Four signed contracts totaling $2 million. A building rising where a pile of junk used to stand.*

It's finite, not ongoing. *We're going to win the final championship—or not. Deficit will turn into surplus—or not.*

It can happen in a reasonable time frame. *This will coincide with the house move and beginning school. We'll wrap it up by the time this outfit celebrates its first anniversary.*

There is a way to measure progress. *We're aiming to cover 250 miles each day. One page of original copy per day. A 10 percent success rate with phone calls, online requests, or related leads.*

It should come as no surprise after reading this list that smaller tasks are easier to execute. When faced with a choice between drafting a business plan or organizing your shoe collection, the deck is stacked in your shoes' favor. The trick is to make the business draft as familiar, as reachable, as doable as laying out your sneakers, slippers, and loafers in a row.

This is especially the case if your taste in footwear requires a thriving stream of revenue. You need to shift the goal (a business plan) away from the abstract and closer to tangible, quick-burst, digestible chunks: a ten-minute race to complete an imperfect outline; a killer opening statement; five minutes of writing your priorities on sticky notes so you stay focused.

In short, you need to be sprinting even if you're committed to a marathon.

ACTION BUILDS BUOYANCY

I was born in 1929, the day after Babe Ruth hit his 500th home run. "Black Tuesday" happened eleven weeks later. On that day, the longest, most severe economic depression ever experienced by the Western industrialized world would start and drag on for ten years. Not a very auspicious start, but my horoscope predicted that I would be "ambitious, confident, loyal, encouraging, and optimistic."

For at least the last sixty years, when people ask me, "How are you, Charlie?" I have replied, "Perfect." It's not necessarily a good or an accurate answer, but it consistently gets attention and provides a starting point for further conversation.

I suppose the clearest way my horoscope's characteristics manifested in my life was in my bias for action over reflection. I like to keep my ambitions simple and clear. I have a flair for making a sport of most anything by getting fired up and pursuing that simple thing like hell.

If I can see the finish line (even if it's only a mental picture), then the path ahead is right where I want to be. My every waking moment is colored by this bias. *Set the table?* I am going to reduce the number of trips by one. *Deliver a toast?* I'll attempt a joke I haven't told before. *Take the garbage out?* I'm going to shave a few seconds off the round-trip time.

It's a rare morning that I don't cut myself shaving because I am so excited about how much I am going to accomplish that day by improving things and pushing the world ever so slightly toward a better version of itself. To make changes that matter, I want to infect others with the confidence and momentum that my simple sprints enable. The truth is, when things are kept simple and moving ahead, everything feels perfect.

The payoff is buoyancy and a greater vitality in dealing with crises and change.

In its simplest form, buoyancy is a measure of spirit, resolve, and positive orientation. While you might argue that events lead people to have positive or negative outlooks, there are numerous studies that have shown the opposite correlation. That is, those who bring a positive disposition to events tend to experience those events (regardless of how others might judge them) as beneficial, important, and enjoyable.

You might say that the world churns around us like a great ocean. But the forces are often only in our heads, restricting us without any basis in reality. In my experience, the truest way to self has been through action, and action is the backbone of my life's story.

FIVE TENETS OF THE PURSUIT MINDSET

It's only now, sixty-five years later, that I can organize my postrace impressions around a basic theme. But my first impressions point to steps that would characterize every significant moment to come. With time, they felt more like leaps, and each situation became more racelike at heart.

Tenet #1: Get clear on what's important
Tenet #2: Find the nearest path forward
Tenet #3: Shift into action
Tenet #4: Don't take no for an answer
Tenet #5: Up the ante

TENET #1: GET CLEAR ON WHAT'S IMPORTANT

The greatest achievements and inspirational stories tend to place an individual's unique nature within situations dependent on resolution and follow-through. For example, we marvel at Helen Keller's triumph over blindness and deafness. Her physiological condition was a factor in her achievement, no doubt. But her desire and moral commitment to living a full life was her extraordinary contribution that made history. Her beliefs triumphed over circumstance.

Before you can do anything of lasting value, you must first get clear on what matters most to you. If you've ever wondered what might tie your various interests and pursuits together, look no further than the values you've explicitly or implicitly reinforced with each of your choices and relationships. As they evolve, so do you and so does your unique life story.

It might be as simple as picking a sport or organizing your room. Both will have some influence on your subsequent opportunities.

Or you might be lucky enough to have your pick of several colleges or find yourself debating between studying for a degree or taking a more vocational path. Both can lead to success if your choice is in sync with a personalized strategy or stems from a part of you that will most naturally stay the course.

If you've ever wondered why others acted against common sense or tradition and yet emerged happier if not more successful, then you've witnessed the power that personal values have on outcomes.

The first tenet says that before you blaze your path you

should revisit your values and principles. Everything stems from them.

Some of the things that strong values do:

- Justify hard-to-explain commitments
- Force and facilitate trade-offs
- Focus on long-term results
- Bring morality and ethics to bear
- Circumnavigate debate
- Provide unity between disparate acts, especially different life stages

But in the end, it is you who must determine how values are defined in your life. What starts out in our less examined youth inevitably tips the scale for good or bad. Developing the skill to understand what's important to you is a vital habit in elevating your efforts from merely dealing with transitions to creating larger change.

TENET #2: FIND THE NEAREST PATH FORWARD

Planning is the skill that makes "on purpose" living possible and a purposeful plan is "values made practical." The aim of *finding the nearest path forward* is to create a synergy between what we do and what we believe.

An interesting example of this is Yvon Chouinard, the lifelong climber and outdoorsman who funded his hobbies early in life by selling custom-designed climbing implements to other sportsmen out of the back of his car. Much of his equipment would set standards of performance while his more novel experiments became standard tools in the modern rock climber's toolkit.

Over time, his personal interests and business ventures merged seamlessly through several companies that eventually became the adventure-gear company Patagonia in 1973. An incredibly mindful and creative leader, he steered through two moral corporate crises that might have toppled a less purposeful business. The first was related to the eroding of rock walls by his climbing implements and the second was over the environmental costs of industrial cotton (a significant ingredient of his catalog).

In both cases, he chose a path forward based on his principles. And in both cases, he was able to shift from cash-generating products and resources toward other offerings that yielded longer-lasting business advantages. He not only earned greater loyalty and more acclaim from customers for his principles, he demonstrated a resolve and an ingenuity that no competitor could claim just as the customer base was becoming more aware about matters of environmental impact.

The point of the second tenet is to ensure that we choose integrity over whim, chance, or disorder.

A good plan will:

- Minimize wasted time and resources
- Ensure that high priorities are tackled first in a smart way
- Communicate the full extent of work in a concise way
- Inspire others to believe in the potential for success

* Ensure that actions combine and converge toward something more meaningful than acting alone

But, most important, it will give you a sense of measurement.

When you peel back my layers, I'm an engineer at heart. In engineering, everything comes back to a universal set of measurements by which a project is benchmarked. Corporate success isn't very different. It's just that we have to be creative in describing the increments of change or quality.

Measurement becomes even more important when groups come together because the effort can easily become abstract, incoherent, or random. Criteria, key performance indicators, milestones, and timing are the spine that holds a high-performance group together. And there's nothing better to build your check-ins and external communications around. After all, it's not only your staff that needs to understand how things are progressing. With big initiatives, you are often at the mercy of public assessment and influencers you might never interact with, much less have a chance to convince. In these instances, measurements that are built in to the fabric of your effort will go a long way to ensure credibility, if not enthusiasm, for your program.

When you periodically measure your efforts, you not only experience motivation but are able to reintegrate what you've learned. As we saw with Yvon Chouinard's example, a person or an organization can create a more sustainable and virtuous cycle of growth. No big change is void of a moral imperative, and support can rarely be obtained without a purpose-led way forward that individuals and groups can commit to.

TENET #3: SHIFT INTO ACTION

Once you're clear on what's important, it's time to blaze your path. The absolute first and most essential step is creating the circumstances in which you are able to do your best work.

You've heard your whole life that time is money and that action is what turns time in our favor because time is what binds things together. Everything you expend energy on is related to how those efforts affect each other. When you're doing things in rapid succession, there's a darn good chance they will add up. But if you yield to sloth, inertia, the status quo, a lack of clarity, or listlessness, that mighty wave aimed at the shore is more likely to disperse into a meaningless froth.

So instead of delaying, try to: *Check the facts. Make a decision. Pick up the phone. Ask a question. Build a model. Share it with others. Give it a pressure test. Measure the outcome.*

The third tenet is about the heart of change: the doing. It means you spend time on what matters—acting, not just preaching; showing up, not silently complaining.

I can't stress enough the importance of knowing your priorities in life. These exist on a personal level (your values). They exist on a project basis (your key outcomes). They exist with respect to your communities (your shared values). The best outcome is when all these layers are sufficiently automatic that your actions are always in line with them.

Sometimes that isn't the case, and you need to be more explicit. Whether you paint them on a wall or e-mail yourself reminders, you need to have your true north always in mind. The alternative is wasted energy and a decreased sense of progress.

TENET #4: DON'T TAKE
NO FOR AN ANSWER

The reason I've focused on action in my life, even to the detriment of planning at times, is that there is an inertia to most things. Problems are abstract until we make them concrete. And nothing firms something up like interaction. In this way, most problems and opportunities are "momentum games." The spoils go to those who get moving sooner and keep moving. Abstraction, concepts, and arguments all bow in the end to what has been done. Focus on momentum. *Keep moving.*

What is also important for maintaining momentum is tackling roadblocks swiftly.

Setbacks will occur. Each one should trigger your creative juices. Sometimes a small tweak to your approach is all that's necessary. In other instances, a whole new frame of reference is needed. Even resolving a small part of a roadblock is progress and maintains momentum. Taking excessive time may make solving a problem easier, but in my experience, this erodes your grasp on the nature of things. Better to stay close to the matter at hand. Better to strike with the proverbial hot iron.

With setbacks, rejection, failure, or changes of circumstance you must keep your response creative and unemotional. When things don't go your way, it's time to pivot and bounce back smarter. As with all the former action you've taken, you can expect your behavior to generate new information, new insights, and quicker alignment with others.

Well-chosen objectives are important, but the most remarkable thing about historic accomplishments is that they
ever came to a conclusion at all. Like negativity in the news,
there's simply more on hand to hold you back or create doubt
than to cheer you on.

A purpose-driven leader thrives on positive reinforce-
ment and has no time for the answer no. Not accepting no
has been fundamental to everything in my life; I don't recognize passive resignation as an option. Consider that the most
successful children's book writer of all time, Dr. Seuss, had
his first book rejected twenty-seven times before he found a
publisher. And consider that the most successful recording
artists of all time, the Beatles, were rejected for a contract
by Decca Records. One of the most celebrated presidents
of the United States, Abraham Lincoln, lost seven elections
before winning the presidency. Legend has it that Disneyland
was turned down 302 times for financing. George Lucas was
turned down by three major studios when he pitched his first
Star Wars movie. And modern entrepreneurs average 3.8 failures before finding success.

In all these cases, success hinged on a single yes. *One* outcome was more powerful, more influential, and more relevant
to history than all the other miscalculations. In each case, the
subjective negative view of possible success was incorrect.
Everyone was guessing. But most guesses come to nothing.
Billie Jean King said, "Losing a tennis match isn't failure, it's
research."

The fourth tenet is about navigating rejection swiftly and
confidently, and not taking it personally. If you've assessed

what's important, found the path, and begun investing your time and the time of others, then no should be given no power over your emotions.

You don't have to be pushy or a jerk, however. You can be assertive without being acidic. The best leaders I've met have managed to balance their creativity and resilience with a respect for others that left all parties feeling more dignified. At the personal level, you'll probably struggle to do that, but in time, your movements will become more automatic, more authentic, and more generous.

Not taking no for an answer doesn't mean stepping on toes or shouting your way to the top of the pack. It does mean:

* Respecting your passion
* Keeping your vision front and center
* Holding the sword loosely
* Staying buoyant

But you have to practice! Growing a thick, friendly skin starts with your most personal experiences. And as with most things, the more you try (and perhaps fail), the more comfortable you become with the instinct to keep pushing forward.

You need to magnify every positive experience and have blinders to setbacks. Don't be that person who counts the cost when things go badly. That thinking can amplify quickly and suffocate the remaining momentum you have toward a goal. You need to be a hoarder of positivity instead. Look for anything that will give your mission energy, confidence, and infectious goodwill.

You mustn't hold on to negatives because they shut down

the very creative abilities that successful tenacity relies on. Make a game of it. Laugh about it with others. Pay attention to and amplify any positives.

While I don't encourage you to weigh your mind down with the possibility of rejection, it's easier for many people if they realize at the outset that acceptance and approval are fundamentally messy to obtain. If you realize that you have to get through twenty noes to get the yes you need, you might start acting sooner and revel in putting the necessary rejections behind you.

Next, you need to embrace a flexible stance. Because getting to yes will throw you into all sorts of situations and negotiations, I've found the samurai concept of *hold the sword loosely* to be very helpful. Instead of coming into discussions with a rigid offer and countering resistance with a repetitive hammering of explanations, the loose sword suggests that you stay true to your offer but be flexible enough to adapt your approach. Holding the sword loosely means leaving room for creativity, for taking note of responses, and for finding new ways of inserting your request into the frame of mind or circumstances of your audience.

TENET #5: UP THE ANTE

A core theme of this book is that the size of the change we can influence depends on our experiences in smaller, more contained domains of change. Like our muscles, we need strong bones to support us. If you want to perform ballet, you'll benefit from the basic discipline of regular exercise.

My run at the Olympics was built on running at a national level. Those wins were built on experiences at the university and high school level. But it would be a mistake to think it was merely physical skill that brought me to the world stage. Planning for training was a talent that evolved from my childhood ventures and was a habit of mine by the time I had entered university to pursue a five-year engineering degree. The engineer's focus on analyzing a chain of events, evaluating the strengths of various elements in the chain, and orienting toward hard data made my thirteen-stride innovation less of a breakthrough and more of a personal passion.

By going full circle in a steadily rising spiral of experience, you won't have to consciously manage every situation. Nor will the number and nature of surprises overwhelm you. That's because—as you spiral upward from one campaign to a more challenging one—you internalize and make automatic the skills employed at that lower level of experience.

Through values, vision, and action, we make transitions progressive. Instead of *retreating* and *resigning*, we learn that transitions can (and should) be moments to up the ante even though outward appearances might suggest otherwise.

IN CONCLUSION

How lucky I am to have known the runner's state of mind, where skill, learning, practice, and effort combine with a flash of energy and creativity to produce the extraordinary burst that enables almost superhuman power and culminates with the thrill of a win.

I feel lucky that all my training came together to produce the privilege of running and winning the Olympic gold. I feel lucky for my past, my rural American roots, and my father's nurturing and intuitive grasp of the path that would enable me to learn and excel. And I feel lucky to have the humility to know when I could not do what I wanted to or hoped for. I developed the ability to go on to the next thing when I recognized a good thing was ending. I have been blessed, then and now, with the legacy of my father's character and his teachings that have been present with me always.

I want you to do everything you can to side with "can do." I want you to never hold back. I want you to explore yourself through positive, authentic action. Central to the notion of resilience is the element of moving quickly toward goals and *gamifying* life. What I call the pursuit mindset encourages you to minimize the hesitation and extended analysis that invite doubt, inertia, and complication.

Now we must turn from the Olympic race to meet the various hurdles I faced later in life and explore the *behavioral* thread that holds a life's various endeavors together.

Chapter 3

INTO THE FIRST TURN

It's what you learn after you know it all that counts.

—ATTRIBUTED TO HARRY S. TRUMAN

It was sixty-five years ago that I traveled as an athlete to the Olympics in Helsinki.

I've never volunteered information about the race or winning the gold medal in the years since. Though I admit many new acquaintances would find out beforehand and ask me to spin a yarn or two. Despite my silence, there were very few moments in my subsequent years that were not anchored or colored by this extraordinary event.

I was young and single-minded, and had few goals beyond competing at the highest level. Within a week, I won a gold medal (the 400-meter hurdles), a silver medal (the 4x400-meter relay), set an Olympic record, and became part of the first father/son Olympic duo to represent the United States in track and field.

The Olympics undeniably added to my confidence.

The Olympics created instant interest in me and established my credibility.

It forever served as the proof that great effort (albeit distributed across a range of less serious spurts) could yield lasting results.

When I crossed the finish line in 1952 I couldn't know any of that. Hell, I could barely form a sentence in my mind. And anyone familiar with hard-earned victories knows the flurry of emotions and thoughts that rush in when the competition is won and you must reengage with the world.

If this had been a team sport, I could've counted on some kind of group catharsis. But this was inevitably more personal and flanked only by adversaries.

Still, the awards ceremony was unfor-

Standing on the podium between Yuriy Lituyev (left) and John Holland (right) during the Olympic flag-raising ceremony.

gettable. The thrill of seeing your own country's flag on the highest pole is unimaginable except for those lucky few who have been there. And I can't forget the pretty blonde Finnish girls bearing the flowers that I later gave to my wife.

David Burghley, an English aristocrat who was the chair of the British Olympic Association and a member of the International Olympic Committee, presented the medals. This was particularly poignant for me because he and my father had both participated in the 1924 Olympics (the Olympics that was featured in the movie *Chariots of Fire*). Lord Burghley had also won the 400-meter hurdles in 1928.

I have never been able to put into words my feelings as my national anthem was played. Maybe it doesn't need words. The memory of it never leaves you.

Awards ceremony with Lord Burghley.

I took the evening off and joined my family and friends on the MS *Batory* in Helsinki harbor. However, I had more races to run so I still had a curfew.

While I was honored to be selected to run the third leg for the United States in the 4x400-meter relay, we lost to Jamaica by one-tenth of a second. Despite our winning the silver medal, this was hard to process as we broke the world record by more than four seconds. This relay was the last race of the XV Olympiad, and we left Helsinki to compete in Sweden and England.

On August 4, 1952, a bank holiday, I ran a 440-yard hurdle race in a U.S. versus British Empire competition in White City Stadium, tying the world record at 0:51.9, with a Brit and a Scot coming in second and third. The next race wasn't scheduled until five days later, so I thought that it was time for a vacation!

My wife, Nancy, and I stuffed ourselves in a small rented VW—along with Walt Ashbaugh, a Cornell classmate who had finished fourth in Helsinki in the triple jump—and headed out of London, determined to get out of the city by nightfall.

There was one serious problem though: Londoners tend to go to the country on bank holidays and they typically go to bed early!

We didn't start looking for a place to spend the night soon enough. In short order, we worked our way down the accommodations ladder to the point where we were seriously inquiring about available jail space!

One thing was certain. All three of us couldn't possibly sleep in the VW!

Desperate, I stopped at a house to see if there was any chance they could provide sleeping space for at least my wife. Walt and I could manage in the car if necessary. By now, most of the houses had turned off their porch lights. I politely knocked on the door of the only house with a porch light still on, and a man came to the door, understood my dilemma, and apologized for not being able to help.

Just then, my Olympic belt buckle glistened in the porch light, and the man asked what it was. When he realized that he was standing in the way of a couple of Olympians getting a good night's sleep, everything changed.

We were invited in, and he and his wife gave Nancy and me their bedroom, even finding a space for the six-foot-four Walt. The next day, fortified with a great English breakfast and overcome by our hosts' generosity, we were ready to drive to Edinburgh—but not before we established a few basic rules of the road: Stop earlier for a place to stay, drive on the left-hand side, and never leave home without our Olympic belts!

Following those rules worked fine; we made it to Edinburgh and played golf, visited museums, and ate a lot of good food all over Scotland, making it back to London the day before the final competition.

On August 9, before a crowd of 50,000 in London's White City Stadium, I won the 440-yard hurdles by 1.1 seconds and set a new world record of 0:51.6, beating Armando Filiput's 1950 record of 0:51.9! Yes, it was drizzling again and the track was very soggy; the sportscasters termed it "puddle jumping."

After what would turn out to be the last race of my career, we were on our way to New York on August 11, and from there, we went by train to Wilmington, Delaware, where lots of well-wishers and family were on hand to tell me of their plans for "Charlie Moore Day." But with only seventeen cents in my pocket, I was more focused on going to work—"on purpose," of course.

As I contemplated my future possibilities, my journey up to this point came flooding back with unsettling speed.

- Racing in the National AAU competition in Madison Square Garden
- Playing "coconut ball" with Jim Fuchs when we were "ambassadors" in Trinidad
- Breaking my own record at the Los Angeles Coliseum
- Graduating from Cornell
- Winning the Olympic tryouts
- Participating in a telethon with Bing Crosby, Dorothy Lamour, and Bob Hope
- Plunging 12,000 feet over Wichita, Kansas, before the pilot was able to restart the engines
- Walking in a ticker-tape parade up Broadway
- Lunching at the Waldorf Astoria
- Flying twenty-three and a half hours to Helsinki
- Skipping the opening ceremonies to focus on the race
- Dining with Prince Philip in Helsinki
- Training with John "Dutch" Holland

It all seemed wonderful and a little unreal.

Each was an accomplishment of its own. But however

swept away I felt, I never considered stopping or even taking time to reflect.

Widely regarded as an athletic innovator who never lost a race in my signature event, I had credentials few athletes in any sport can claim.

Yet I gave up racing and embraced a completely different path the next year. It would be one of the many dramatic shifts in a life defined by inspired action and constant reintegration of experiences into exciting new forms of success.

SETTING ASIDE THE MEDAL

Do I count the Olympics as the biggest thing I've done in my life?

If you use fame as the measurement, I would have to say yes.

But if you measure it against the things I would take on later with others, then no. The Olympics were only one of the many satisfying events in my life.

Given my dramatic win in Helsinki, many people wondered why I stopped competing in track to work in something as mundane as a family business.

But the real and recurring test of *resilience* is with our *transitions* in life and how we move from a place of comfort to a place of new potential.

Sports and fame weren't at the core of my self-image. I was proud of them, but they did not define my full path. In their place, I had values, behaviors, and a character that let me deeply engage in something without getting stuck.

They helped me embrace change and move swiftly into an unknown future wholly my own. They kept me honest.

You can turn anything into a game by embracing the shift from one pursuit to the next. I moved on from the 1952 Olympics and continued to race in pursuit of:

- Education
- Family
- Turnarounds
- The arts
- Giving back
- The greater good of business

Sheer luck certainly plays a large role when opportunities fall into your lap. But serendipity is more often than not the result of seeds that were planted long ago. When you live a life governed by your values, when every choice you make comes from your personal truths, you draw the right things toward yourself.

My career after the Olympics has been a series of leaps from one position to the next. It is part of our family lore that we moved sixteen times in forty-four years. While some of my moves were carefully calculated, most of them came to me without my prompting. Had I not remained open to things, I might have lost out on some of the more important opportunities in my career and some of the best times for my family.

Life is filled with opportunities. Finding the best way forward comes from scrutinizing new opportunities according to your values and taking flying leaps when your heart says yes.

In 1952 I had gold around my neck and fire in my belly. But I couldn't stay twenty-two forever. My thirteen-stride technique wouldn't help me off the track. But I was committed to using the attitude that had invented those thirteen steps in everything I would be a part of from that day forward. From here on out, everything would be characterized by drive, determination, optimism, focus, hard work, and grit. My horoscope had uncannily come true.

But even though I moved on from the 1952 Olympics, I didn't stop racing. I was now sprinting toward new challenges and becoming more concerned with how we compete (and win) as teams, organizations, and communities.

Chapter 4

WHERE IT ALL BEGAN

Do not train children to learn by force or harshness,
but direct them to it by what amuses their minds, so that
you may be better able to discover with accuracy the
peculiar bent of the genius of each.

—PLATO

IMMUTABLE INFLUENCES

One of my secret joys in meeting new people is hearing their unique stories about how they got to where they are. And I enjoy sensing the power they draw from their families, friends, and community. There are no stereotypes about upbringing that stand up for long when you look at all the variables that shaped (and still influence) a person. Who you are is a direct reflection of your experiences. And for many people, the deepest set of connected experiences comes from where they grew up.

I know today that the land where I grew up and the people I came from bracket my later, more cosmopolitan life and remind me that my roots are dug deep. My origins and the locales of my life have had an important effect on my nature and development. My childhood was a typical—and lucky—all-American life mixed with the grit and warmth of my family history and personal geography. I grew in the soil of decency, hard work, and American forthrightness. Here was a place with strength of character, a solidity, a simplicity, and a respect for people and the land.

I chose my forebears well. I am grounded in American values, the rock-solid ethos of constancy, optimism, achievement, and regard for the lives of others, of trust, clarity, and responsibility. When I won the Olympic race and stood proudly in view of the U.S. flag, I felt then (and feel now) that I am an American through and through. While I was extremely honored and proud to represent my country at the Olympics, my nation was not the only thing on my mind, nor did my feelings drift to my college or prep school although both made great contributions to my development. What did dominate my thoughts was my family, especially my father, who played a critical role in my life and certainly taught me to "run on purpose."

This realization of the central role my family played in my life has been a continuing thread through all of my later endeavors. My father was the one who brought me to the starting line of my life, the "get set" point. He inspired a coach to turn me into a runner. He inspired me with enthusiasm and the realization that I could exploit my raw material and do something with it.

It took application, of course, and practice, grit, and extreme concentration, and also inspiration and the desire to win. Dad communicated all of this to me in the most caring and gentle of ways. Then I took off, and what a run it has been.

Because of my father's example and urging, I learned to take advantage of opportunities and never give up!

MY GRANDFATHER: DOCTOR, LEADER, CIVIC ACTIVIST

My maternal grandfather, Dr. S. Horace Scott, was born just outside Coatesville, Pennsylvania, on March 23, 1865, and died at the age of eighty-seven on July 13, 1952, eight days before I won my gold medal in Helsinki.

My grandfather embodied the spirit and humanitarian values that went with the life he carved out for himself as a country doctor with a black bag and horse and buggy. And he kept the public good always in his sights as he engaged in numerous civic activities and served on local boards.

Horace Scott's engagement to Annie Chandler Scarlett was announced on November 14, 1890, with their wedding taking place four days later (according to the customs of the Society of Friends). The local papers described the ceremony as the "social event of the season." My grandmother was the daughter of Joel Scarlett, who was described as a "wealthy and honored citizen."

My grandfather Scott at Wake Robin, a summer cottage that he built in 1910.

Dr. and Mrs. Scott had three children, Margaret, Jane (my mother), and Horace.

Jane Scott and my father were married in Holy Trinity Episcopal Church in Coatesville on June 28, 1928.

I came along less than fourteen months later. With my maternal grandmother's passing earlier in 1928, my parents decided to live with Dr. Scott in the big stone house on the corner of Third Avenue and Chestnut Street where I was raised until I was eight and my sister Anne was three.

Grandfather Scott maintained his offices in that house until he officially retired in 1946. The premises were complete with a separate entrance, a waiting room, and closets with skeletons! What fun I had scaring my friends who visited! While the horse-and-buggy era had passed, there was a stable and a garage in the back along with a sandbox and a swing—recent additions for me and my sister to play on. In addition to my grandfather's offices, the first floor included a large parlor, living and dining rooms, a spacious kitchen, and numerous pantries.

There were enough bedrooms on the second floor to accommodate us all plus a sitting room. My room was next to the stairs to the attic, a cavernous assortment of rooms that held every manner of "stuff": antique clothes, Civil War relics, anything and everything to fascinate a kid! This was the idyllic life I was fortunate to have for eight years. There could not be a more enchanting, magical environment to grow up in.

My family's forge shop was on the banks of the Brandywine south of Coatesville and north of Chadds Ford. During

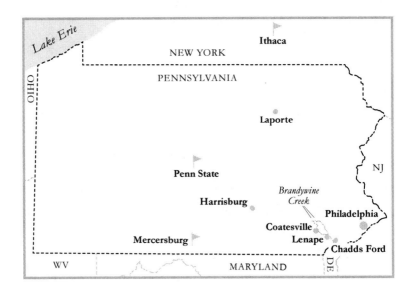

World War II, the realist artist Andrew Wyeth used to paint there in the winter to get out of the cold. There are still neighbors who can remember the year (circa 1940) when the Brandywine froze solid with twelve inches of black ice, and people could literally ice-skate from Coatesville to Wilmington—typical lore of the Brandywine Valley!

MOVING TO A NEW HOME

In the spring of 1938 my family moved from Coatesville to Wawaset near the banks of Brandywine Creek. Our new home, Edgewood (where my baby brother, Tom, was born that August), had a charming house, a springhouse, a root cellar, a chicken house, a stable, and a stream-fed pool. My parents lived there until they retired to Florida in their late sixties. It was a great place to grow up!

My family at Edgewood circa 1940.
I am standing in the back and my sister,
Anne, and brother, Tom, are seated in
the foreground.

The Brandywine's sinuous undulations and rolling greenswards embody harmony, solace, and the poetry of nature—qualities worthy of Walt Whitman or the Brandywine School of artists. Who better than Andrew Wyeth to paint this timeless land inhabited by the Lenape Indians, early Swedish settlers, and Quakers speaking in "plain" language with quiet but solid values.

MY FATHER: THE ONE AND ONLY "CRIP"

My father was Charles H. Moore, Sr. (1901–1983). His father, Fred E. Moore (1877–1934), owned a one-third interest in the Coatesville Boiler Works, whose employ he had entered at the age of seventeen. In 1923 Fred and others founded the Lenape Hydraulic Pressing & Forging Company after my grandfather disagreed with his former partners about the design of a new boiler.

As a boy, my father hunted and fished with his father and was very active in a local YMCA summer camp. He spent nine summers there, first as a camper and then as a counselor. It was at Camp Chesapeake that he nearly cut off his right toe stepping on a mussel shell in low tide and picked up the moniker "Crippled," which was later shortened to "Crip," a nickname that stuck with him for the rest of his life.

In Coatesville High School, Dad lettered in football, basketball, baseball, swimming, and track—his favorite. He captained the team and anchored their winning mile-relay team at the Penn Relays in 1920.

It was in this high school that he met and fell in love with my mother.

Dad was not a great student so, to improve his study

skills, his father sent him and his younger brother, Ted (Fred, Jr., 1902–1953), to Mercersburg Academy, a preparatory boarding school founded in 1893 in Mercersburg, Pennsylvania. It was about 150 miles west of Coatesville and 90 miles northwest of Washington, D.C.

He went there for his senior year and took a year as a post-graduate student while my uncle Ted attended for his junior and senior years.

In the summer, my father worked as a draftsman at the Coatesville Boiler Works, which was struggling financially so much so that Dad gave up his dream to go to Cornell and got a full scholarship to Penn State for both himself and Ted.

My father eventually joined my grandfather's new venture, the Lenape Hydraulic Pressing & Forging Company, and my uncle Ted taught English and coached at Saint James Academy in Maryland until he joined his brother and father in the fledgling family business. My grandfather was the vice president and treasurer of Lenape; and the president of the company, Charles Fairbrother, was very knowledgeable about manufacturing, but he had two weaknesses, women and drink, and he was ultimately fired. The other two investors left within a few years. This is where my father started to make a difference as he faced lagging sales and the difficulty of financing new orders.

My father was a larger-than-life character. Full of spark and vigor, he was an extrovert who was proud, kind, generous, and creative (he owned many patents). "Crip" Moore was an outdoorsman and an excellent cook who was warm, vital, and devoted to his family. Above all, he never let the truth stand in the way of a good story. He was a real guy and his grandchildren adored him.

FATHER AND SON: PARALLEL PATHS

Dad was my mentor and my very best friend. It was a relationship forged of love and respect. It doesn't get better than that.

As I look back over our unique relationship, there are many similarities between us, many parallel paths, and many shared experiences.

My father and I were both born in Coatesville. Both of us attended Coatesville schools and Mercersburg Academy. We even went to the same YMCA camp on the Chesapeake Bay! And both of us were captains of our track teams in prep school and college. I was initially interested in going to Penn State but enrolled at Cornell instead while my father wanted to go to Cornell and ended up attending Penn State.

We were the first U.S. father and son to have been on Olympic teams that competed in track and field, and we both set world records in the hurdles. Our joint achievements were recognized in 2001 when we were honored with the inaugural Steinbrenner Family Heritage award that recognizes multi-generational ties in the Penn Relays.

A TOUGH ACT TO FOLLOW

Dad's first two years running for Penn State were spectacular: he won the 120-yard high hurdles at the Penn Relays in 15.4 seconds in 1923 and the 120-yard high-hurdle title in 15.2 at the prestigious Intercollegiate Association of Amateur Athletes of America (IC4A) championships in 1924. He set the world record of 8.6 seconds when he won the 70-yard high hurdles in the IC4A indoor championships that year in New York.

All the stars were aligned for him to qualify for one of the four spots on the 1924 U.S. Olympic team in the 110-meter high hurdles. (That number was reduced to three in 1932.) Dad's dream of gold, however, was not to be; in the finals, my father hit the ninth and tenth hurdles, miraculously keeping his stride but finishing fifth. Even so, the Olympic coaches elected to take the first five finishers, likely taking into account my father's domination of hurdling titles that year.

My father and I in our Olympic uniforms.

The plan was to run a time trial in Paris to determine which four athletes would represent the U.S. in the VIII Olympiad. But an international ruling on the eve of the first heats of the 110-meter high hurdles declared that the athletes had to qualify in the order they finished in the U.S., not in Paris. This ruling made my father the alternate while his four teammates, George Guthrie of Ohio State (who would finish third but be disqualified for knocking over three hurdles), Dan Kinsey of Illinois (who would win with a time of 15.0 compared to my father's earlier time of 15.2), Pitch Johnson of Illinois (who would not make the finals), and Karl Anderson of Minnesota (who would finish fifth), went on to compete in the Paris Olympics.

My father was devastated. Yes, he had made the team, a goal he had set for himself three years before. Yes, he had an incredible experience sailing to Paris on a ship with luminaries such as Douglas Fairbanks, Jr. But it was difficult for him to sit in the stands and know in his heart that he should be competing on the track.

My father did have an opportunity after the Olympics to compete in some exhibition matches in Sweden and England, where the U.S. team of Guthrie, Kinsey, Anderson, and Dad (who ran the third leg) won a 4x120-yard shuttle hurdle race with a time of 61.6 on July 19, 1924, but after that, it was time for my father to head home.

RESPECTIVE STUMBLES WE OVERCAME

One day before my sixth birthday, I was chasing a friend across Third Avenue and was run over by a car and suffered a serious leg fracture. My mother heard the screeching of tires, saw me lying in the street, and raced down from a bedroom on the second floor, leaving my half-clad younger sister in the bassinet. My sister survived being abandoned, but it took me much longer to recover as pins and other devices weren't successful in knitting the broken bones. So the doctors resorted to lacing them together with kangaroo gut. Years later, this made a great story for sportscasters. I was in the hospital for so long that I forgot how to tie my shoelaces, a real liability for a kid just heading to school.

In 1924, right after returning from the Olympics, my father also experienced a serious accident that would hinder his athletic career.

After returning from Paris, Dad started working in his father's start-up business. My grandfather and his partners were converting an old power plant on a branch line of the Reading railway to manufacture components for boilers and other metal tanks. They had installed vintage presses from 1890 along with lathes, shears, pumps, and electric welding equipment. My father planned to work at the new facility until college started in the fall.

A few weeks later, Dad was standing next to a seventy-five-ton C-press with his right hand resting on the press plate while he gestured with the other when a faulty valve caused the press to close on the four fingers of his right hand.

The doctors at the hospital told him that his fingers could be saved but that he would have little or no use of them. My father said that his fingers should be removed if they were going to be useless. The surgery that left him with a palm and a thumb was undertaken successfully, but the mental recovery was a challenge.

He was a world record holder and an Olympian with a bright athletic career ahead of him! How could he now take his marks at the start of a race? How could he write? What was his future?

The healing of his hand progressed rapidly; the healing of his spirit and self-confidence took more time. His best therapy was playing golf, which he accomplished by ingeniously strapping his club to both hands with a leather thong. This physical exercise was critical to his recovery, as was the satisfaction of succeeding. In no time, he taught himself to hold a pen or pencil between his right thumb and the stub of his hand in a way that enabled him to print better than most people could.

He reported to college a little late, but he insisted on reporting to track practice. His coach suggested that he "hang it up." My father refused on the grounds that he was the captain-elect and thought he could score points in dual meets. With that, his coach took him to the University of Pennsylvania where they fitted him with a special glove so he could balance himself when taking his marks.

It took a lot of practice, but in his junior year, despite all that had happened over the last nine months, he won the 120-yard high hurdles in the Penn Relays with a time of 14.8, his best time ever. In the semifinals of the IC4As where he was the defending champion, he lost his stride when he struck the next-to-last hurdle in the semifinals and failed to qualify for the final although he did place third in the low hurdles.

In his senior year, he placed third in the high hurdles and fifth in the lows (George Steinbrenner's father was third) at the IC4As. In addition, he anchored a winning shuttle hurdle relay race in 1926 in the Penn Relays and placed in the Millrose and New York Athletic Club games, along with scoring a lot of points in dual meets, where Penn State was undefeated.

NOTABLE DIFFERENCES

Despite how closely my life tracked with my father's, there were differences. For example, my father loved to gamble. While I have no time for gambling in any form, my father's genes rolled over to at least one of his grandchildren. Dad would take my six-year-old son David to Delaware Park to play the ponies. David would later claim that this introduction to horse racing and gambling greatly helped his math skills!

On the occasions that Dad won, he would put David to work counting the take, and if my father lost, David would have a great luncheon with his grandmother while his grandfather shuttled back and forth between the paddock and the betting windows.

If my father was silent when he returned from the track, we assumed that he had lost. But when he won big, he was eager to share the largesse, spreading hundred-dollar bills on the dining-room table and saying, "Charlie, is this enough to build that three-acre farm pond or add the eating porch to the cottage?"

I wish that Dad could have lived to see David's horse, Pollard's Vision, run in the Kentucky Derby! Or to watch one of Pollard's Vision's major wins in a pounding rainstorm with jockey Jerry Bailey on board. It seems that running in the rain is a family tradition.

THE VISIONARY AND THE
PROJECT MANAGER

My father encouraged me to own and ride horses. Our deal was that he would buy the horses and I would do all the work and find a way to raise money to feed them. I did get to experience the thrill of the fox chase and won blue ribbons in the "handy hunter" event at weekend horse shows, but I came to accept that this enjoyable sport was possible only after satisfactorily completing my responsibilities.

My mother felt strongly that the care of my animals was my job. And I credit her with instilling a strong work ethic in me from an early age. I had to earn money for feeding, shoeing, and transporting the horses. I raised hundreds of day-old chicks to the fryer stage then killed and dressed them to sell to my mother's friends.

My parents called this "learning responsibility," and my father was a good teacher. I worked with Fred Lewis, a handyman hired by my father, and learned how to wield a scythe, a crosscut saw, and a digging iron as I became the project manager for my father's ideas.

Making a game of my responsibilities became a habit of mine. And the game kept getting bigger, more elaborate, and more satisfying. For example:

- Breaking the ice in a nearby stream to collect water without spilling it all over your school clothes
- Feeding and watering both chickens and horses twice a day, as well as exercising the horses
- Working our two vegetable gardens in the spring and summer

Jumping a different kind of hurdle in a horse show circa 1944.

When I was a teenager, Tom Dewey ran against Franklin Roosevelt for the presidency. A neighbor of ours was the county chair of the Republican Party and had a number of big campaign buttons to distribute. He asked me if I would take them to Lenape Park, a somewhat down-on-its-heels amusement park located on Brandywine Creek.

FDR was very popular at that time, so I was somewhat timid when distributing buttons for the New York governor who was challenging him—not to mention that I knew nothing about politics. Suddenly, a man came up and offered to pay me one dollar for a button. I had a stack of them to give away, but my entrepreneurial spirit got the best of me and I agreed to the sale.

Nearby observers rushed up and wanted the same deal,

and suddenly, I was in business until I sold all the buttons! When I returned home and recounted this story to my father, he had two reactions: pride in my entrepreneurialism and disappointment in my willingness to sell the buttons I was supposed to give away.

The solution: I rode my horse to the county chair's farm and made my first political contribution—the proceeds of my Lenape Park bonanza!

One day, Dad said, "Charlie, it's time for you to go to Mercersburg. You know, that's what turned me from a raw boy into a man." It is true that I had been missing more and more school so I could foxhunt during the week, and maybe I was ready to go away to school. Still, it meant selling the horses and folding up my chicken business, not to mention leaving my special parents and my twelve-year-old sister and seven-year-old brother.

MY MOTHER:
THE CALM CHEERLEADER

My mother was three years younger than my father and the youngest of the three Scott siblings. She was a good athlete in high school and played on the varsity basketball team. She taught school for one year in Coatesville after graduating from Goucher College in Towson, Maryland.

Mother seemed quite comfortable living in the country, possibly because she was an avid reader. And there was always lots of canning and freezing to do. One of my favorite memories of my mother was helping her to preserve strawberries from our garden and the wild ones we picked along the road. We did this by using large platters under glass, which was my introduction to the power and effectiveness of solar energy. I still have one of those great pottery platters!

MOTHER'S STOIC CARETAKING

My relationship with my mother was different from the close connection I had with my father. It was more familial, less

My mother, Jane Scott Moore, 1925.

businesslike. From the time I left for Mercersburg, I was more of a visitor in our home, notwithstanding the love I had for my parents and siblings. I was introverted and very focused, a veneer that only my father easily penetrated.

Mother worried over and cared for me following my broken leg surgery and when I had my tonsils removed at the age of eight. Even though I apparently ran away from home several times and experienced some difficulty in reading aloud, my mother persevered. She always supported my raising chickens and caring for my horses. One day, I talked her into riding in my horse-drawn sleigh behind an old gray mare that didn't have much experience with the gear. The same thing was true for the driver!

Almost at once, Smoky the horse got spooked by the cupping of snow against the sleigh and away we went in a dead run! All the strength I could muster in pulling up the reins was ineffective, and I had no idea what Smoky would do when we arrived at the spot where the road dead-ended at Brandywine Creek. We soon found out: Smoky abruptly stopped and looked around as if to ask, *What do we do now?* All I can remember is that my mother and I were very scared and relieved when Smoky decided to stop!

A NEW ERA FOR LENAPE FORGE

As I was growing up, the undercapitalized family business continued to struggle. My grandfather Moore started to let his life insurance policies lapse in order to help finance the business. When he died, he was broke and in debt, and the company owed him fifteen weeks of back pay. Grandfather Moore died in 1934, and I vividly remember trying to console my father as he lay on his bed in Grandfather Scott's house prostrate with grief.

In the meantime, my uncle Cardy (Richard Carvell, 1908–1985) had given up his osteopathic practice in New Jersey to join the family business. My father, who was already the president of Lenape Forge, arranged for his mother to serve as "general manager" so she could have some income after my grandfather died. In a few years, the youngest brother, Gerry (Gerald S., 1922–1975), would join my father, Uncle Ted, and Uncle Cardy in the business as production manager.

Although Gerry attended one year at Penn State, he had virtually no training for his new responsibilities.

REBUILDING DESPITE A SHAKY FOOTING

From the beginning, there were disagreements between the four brothers that were exacerbated by the fact that my grandmother felt strongly that each son should have equal equity in the company despite the fact that her two older sons had initially taken company stock in lieu of pay. This was not unusual in those days. My father, who made it a point to be close to all of the employees by hunting, fishing, shooting darts, and drinking beer with them as well as attending their weddings and funerals, often had to get employees to work seven days a week while only paying them for two days until the company could afford to pay back wages. The company struggled through the Depression but eventually paid off all its past debts.

At the time my grandfather Moore died, the Sun Shipbuilding & Drydock Company accounted for as much as 50 percent of Lenape Forge's sales. Dad went to the head of their pressure vessel division and explained the situation; he was then introduced to Arthur Pew, the president of Sun Oil, who handed my father a check for $25,000 to cover future orders with a 5 percent discount and expressed his gratitude for Lenape being such a dependable supplier. No written agreement was necessary, just a friendly handshake!

The Moore boys weren't all business and family feuds.

Cardy owned and bred racehorses. Gerry, with the encouragement of his mother, got into the Thoroughbred racehorse business in a big way. Grandmother Moore was always very good to me, sending me her special cookies when I was at Mercersburg, but the greatest treat of all was her taking me to Eachus Dairies for strawberry ice cream! Grandmother Moore died in 1954, and the company's stock was divided equally among her three remaining sons. Throughout this trying time, my dad managed to maintain his equilibrium.

BECOMING A BUSINESSMAN

While I had spent several summers working in the plant at Lenape and had done some testing of Lenape products in the Cornell lab, I had actively pursued other engineering positions, which were very scarce in 1952. As I approached graduation (and the Helsinki Olympics), I had gotten two offers I was really excited about: one from Bethlehem Steel and one from DuPont. I sat down with my father to discuss my options, and Dad was very straightforward. "Look, Charlie, I have gotten you this far; now I need your help in running our family business." Of course, I said, "Yes, sir," and I never looked back.

THE BLOOD WASN'T ALL THAT THICK

While I was in school and competing in track meets around the world, the family dynamics at Lenape Forge weren't improving. And now here I was, adding another generation to a complicated family business. But what I had going for me was a real passion to help the business and advance our product lines and capabilities. I was first in to the office and last out. I had to learn to avoid interfering in my uncles' "domains," but that wasn't too difficult because there was so much to do that no one else was doing. I had the run of the shop, and I loved it!

New products and new customers helped as Lenape took on more sophisticated applications and metallurgical challenges. New sales agencies opened new doors. The business, while all-consuming for Dad and me, was still very small, and Dad was itching to sell it. The differences in styles, work habits, and interests among the three owners weren't the only problem; there was also no appreciation on the part of some family members for what the others were doing or contributing, and my father continued to push to sell the business.

By now, my kid brother, Tom, who had graduated from Mercersburg in 1957 and was attending Penn State, joined the Lenape salesforce, where he ended up making a real difference. But we still needed more business! So Dad and I started pursuing more customers and a possible buyer for Lenape.

My uncles seemed to be ambivalent about our divestiture plans, but they did want a lot of money to give up their "cushy" jobs. I had negotiated options to buy their stock, and those options were about to expire. We were running out of time to find a buyer for Lenape, but our attempts to find one bore no fruit until we piqued the interest of Bonney Forge, a company we supplied various products to. Bonney was owned by Miller Manufacturing, a company that had just been acquired by Gulf+Western, a growing conglomerate that would eventually acquire Paramount Studios and other sizeable operations.

Despite the fact that my father and I were unsuccessful in negotiating with the G+W accountants, I went to New York in 1965 to try one more avenue. Returning to my hotel that night, I found a note pinned to my door stating that Charles Bluhdorn, the chairman of G+W, would like to see me the next morning in his office—on a Saturday, no less!

I had spent about ten minutes highlighting the Lenape business and five minutes on the proposed deal when Bluhdorn interrupted me, and said, "Charlie, I like you and I believe in you. Subject to our visit to your operations, I will agree to your uncles' terms and will negotiate with your father in terms of G+W stock. Do we have a deal? We can close in sixty days." There was no paperwork, just a warm handshake.

As it happened, Bluhdorn and a G+W executive, David "Jim" Judelson, visited Lenape less than two weeks later and the deal was closed shortly after.

I was named the president of Lenape; Dad became the chairman. When the G+W executives had visited Lenape for their first and only time, they had asked me where I wanted to take the business. I explained my dream for entering the nuclear-component arena and what that would require, adding that I had already identified the used equipment and building, then being torn down, to complete this expansion. They were ecstatic and approved my project on the spot with only one caveat: double the size of the building! So we did.

AFTER THE SALE

It was great fun building on the dreams I had for the family business, and I believe we succeeded. As G+W grew, the Lenape Forge division kept being shuffled down the organizational structure, but we still had the full support of the various levels of hierarchy because we had earned it. And my brother became our sales manager and then took on additional sales responsibility in divisions and subsidiaries above Lenape Forge.

Years later, my son David graduated from Cornell's business school and became a well-respected equity analyst who was best known for his extensive coverage of conglomerates—including Gulf+Western!

When David was interviewed about who would take over following Chairman Bluhdorn's fatal heart attack, he predicted that the new CEO would be Jim Judelson. Twelve hours later, Martin Davis, an entertainment executive who was their executive vice president, was anointed president and CEO. Over the next decade, David was constantly reminded of his mistake by Davis!

In 1973, I had fulfilled my dreams at Lenape, and after twenty years, it was time to move on. I was recruited by the executive search firm Heidrick & Struggles to run Interpace Corporation's Lapp Insulator Division in LeRoy, New York. I was excited about my new job, but I regretted leaving the people Dad and I had depended on at Lenape.

Dad stayed on at Lenape until 1975—over fifty years in the business! He never stopped inventing and continued to manage his patents, many of which were directly related to Lenape products and processes. He didn't hesitate to sue when he felt his rights were being infringed on.

MY FATHER'S FINAL YEARS

In time, Dad started writing short stories about his life to share primarily with his grandchildren. He also took creative writing courses at a local community college. He never grew tired or gave up on the things he loved: business, fun, and family. He was a tremendous example of how invigorating it is to be swept up in one's pursuits.

My father died in 1983. I got the call about his death when I was in the middle of negotiations to acquire Interpace, the company I left Lenape Forge to work for ten years earlier. It's a small world even in business! I felt as if my father were just checking in with me, as he always had. After all, he was my father, my mentor, and my best friend. He departed this world as a result of a heart attack on the golf course. What a way to go! He crowded at least 182 years of life into his 82 years on earth and left us a legacy to respect.

Chapter 5

HIGHER LEARNING

Aim for success, not perfection. Never give up your right to be wrong, because then you will lose the ability to learn new things and move forward with your life.

—DAVID D. BURNS

TOWARD FINDING MY PURPOSE

I was raised to expect I'd go away to boarding school when the time was right. That was what my father had done so why would I not follow in his footsteps? I believed that going away to school was an enormous privilege, however, not a given. The purpose was to prepare yourself for your life's journey by getting the best possible education, interacting with the best possible faculty and students, and engaging in other activities that would enhance the overall experience.

But there was one problem. My "purpose" was not yet clear. Did it have to do with animals? Would it lead to business? What were my options?

I was thankful that I had parents I respected and trusted, and I was willing to do what they suggested, which served me well.

I could not have found better educational institutions than Mercersburg Academy and Cornell University. Both schools helped me find my way and purpose as I built my self-confidence, developed a work ethic, coped with seemingly abstract things, and learned to compete in the classroom, on the athletic field, and in the wider world.

MERCERSBURG ACADEMY'S PROUD SPORTS HISTORY

When Dr. William Mann Irvine arrived on the Mercersburg campus in 1893, organized sports programs at American educational institutions were still in their infancy. Irvine, the school's twenty-eight-year-old founding headmaster and a graduate of Phillips Exeter Academy, Princeton University, and the Theological Seminary of the Reformed Church in Lancaster, Pennsylvania, had different ideas about how to blend and enhance scholarship and athletics.

The powerful bond between athlete and coach has always been a paramount strategy of Mercersburg's sports programs. It's all about pride, mutual trust, hard work, and the willingness to listen and learn, just as it is in the classroom.

The school has produced fifty-four Olympians to date

(primarily in track and swimming), including thirteen medalists, who have earned twelve golds, five silvers, and four bronzes.

As we came into view of the magnificent chapel at Mercersburg, my father turned to me, and said, "You know, Charlie, at Mercersburg, you address all professors and elders as 'sir.'" I said, "Yes, sir," and I never again addressed my father in any other manner. It was a powerful moment for me, the beginning of my journey to adulthood. I am also proud of the fact that all six of my sons show the same respect even though only three of them attended Mercersburg.

JIMMY CURRAN: COACH, MENTOR, LEGEND

Jimmy Curran served as track coach at Mercersburg for fifty-one years, from 1910 to 1961. The witty Scotsman was born in Galashiels in 1880, ran the mile as an amateur and later as a pro, and won the Irish championship in 1903.

Jimmy came to America on the ill-fated *Lusitania* in 1907 and went to work in a steel mill; later, he got a job as a "rubber" (an important form of physical therapy) at the University of Pennsylvania until Dr. Irvine employed him in 1910.

His greatest thrill was coaching Ted Meredith when he won the Olympic 800-meter event in 1912, the first Mercersburg schoolboy to become an Olympic champion.

Curran's ready wit and ability to tell a good yarn endeared him to thousands of Mercersburg boys, and his shrewd common sense helped him train some outstanding track men during his illustrious career.

The stories told about him at the academy are legendary. For example, he could drop-kick a goal from the thirty-yard line in his bare feet and send the ball flying for fifty yards. On one occasion, the "indestructible" Scotsman played 290 holes of golf on the academy course between five a.m. and eight p.m. on a hot summer day. He played the whole round with a three iron and claimed that he started with three balls and ended with five!

Jimmy lived in the village of Mercersburg with his wife, also a native of Scotland; they had four children. He died on February 7, 1963, of a coronary occlusion.

There was no question that my father always wanted me to follow in his steps at Mercersburg. When he introduced me to Curran, Jimmy said, "Your dad was a hurdler; let's see if we can make you a hurdler." Truth is, I had never run competitively before, so it was a big deal to teach me the required three steps between the high hurdles, let alone get me over those three-foot-six-inch-high barriers!

OTHER MERCERSBURG INFLUENCES AND FRIENDS

I made some lifetime friends at Mercersburg, including Will Allen (my roommate both years), Skip Fidler (from Canada), Bill Arnold (from Colorado), "Brooklyn" Jones (from guess where), and Jack Tanger (from York, Pennsylvania). I was also fortunate to begin a lifetime friendship with Joe Strode (from West Chester, Pennsylvania). Joe and I teamed up to win some of the most exciting golf matches over the next twenty-five years. In 1972, we traveled with the Strode family and three of our children around Europe and attended the Munich Games together.

As captivating as Coach Curran was, there was also an amazing group of faculty members. All of them were true educators and mentors.

My French teacher, Mr. Montgomery, mostly addressed me as *"Mon Dieu!,* Moore." My favorite English teacher, "Snag" Smith, was also a savvy dorm proctor; he could streak down the dorm hall with only one shoe on and arrive at your room much sooner than you expected!

A SNAPSHOT OF LIFE AT MERCERSBURG

Mercersburg became co-ed in 1969. Before that, Penn Hall and Wilson College, both women's schools in nearby Chambersburg, were popular sources for dates.

We had debating and public speaking on Saturday mornings and did a fair amount of traveling for track. Our track team was undefeated in our senior year, and I had the good fortune to win the prestigious Williams Cup by one-half of a point!

At Mercersburg, I had the opportunity to grow up, to prove that I could study and interact with faculty, to run and even captain my track team, and to follow the rules. But it was a miracle that I did not receive even one hour of guard duty, the punishment for any infraction of those rules.

My father presenting me with the Williams Cup at Mercersburg Academy in 1947, with the head of school and my track coach seated in the background.

A MERCERSBURG BOY FOR LIFE

I graduated cum laude, placing ninth in a class of 147. My first college acceptance came from Dartmouth and was followed by Cornell, Lafayette, and Penn State. But my journey with Mercersburg didn't end with graduation.

From 1996 to 2005, I had the honor of serving on the Board of Regents for three terms, including chairing the very successful Mightily Onward capital campaign. We raised $138 million for the endowment and capital projects, far greater than the school's previous best of $27 million. A great example of balancing a big vision with a string of tireless sprints.

In 1972 the outdoor running track at Mercersburg was named in honor of Coach Jimmy Curran; and in 1993 the recalibration and resurfacing of this track was dedicated to my father.

In 2002 I was honored with the Class of '32 Plaque, Mercersburg's highest alumni award.

I have been privileged to speak at graduation twice, including for my son Brian's graduating class in 1994.

When I contributed my two Olympic medals to Mercersburg, I did so by saying, "I owe everything in my track career to Jimmy Curran, who simply turned to this kid who had never run before—ever—and said, 'Here, let me help you.'"

Father and son graduation photos from Mercersburg Academy—twenty-five years apart!

WHY CORNELL?

I had followed my father to Mercersburg; why not to his alma mater, Penn State, where I had also been accepted for admission? I had even gone there the summer before my freshman year for a week of training. But because of the great influx of returning veterans, many taking advantage of the GI Bill, Penn State wasn't taking freshmen on their main campus. And Cornell's engineering program, one of the best in the country, was a five-year program so I would be finishing my studies in time for the 1952 Summer Olympics (what a wild dream!). I had the good fortune to attend this great university with the intent to "learn on purpose" in more ways than one!

Both of my parents were completely supportive of my tackling the five-year mechanical engineering program at Cornell. The fact that I was a walk-on athlete with no scholarship of any kind was not a negative factor.

The fact that Jack Moakley, Cornell's widely respected track coach, was retiring soon didn't seem to bother my father or me; I already had a coach—my father. He was terrific with my teammates; they treated him as a father and coach as well. My father also carried on a regular correspondence with the New York sportswriters, which could prove embarrassing and always heaped more pressure on me.

JACK MOAKLEY

Jack Moakley served as the head coach of Cornell's cross-country and track and field teams for fifty years, from

1899 to 1949. His record at Cornell is impressive: twenty-nine IC4A championships, twenty-five Olympians, and coaching the U.S. track and field team in the 1920 Olympic Games in Antwerp. He was elected to the Cornell Sports Hall of Fame in its inaugural year, 1978, and to the National Track and Field Hall of Fame in 1988.

Even though Moakley was nearing retirement when I entered Cornell in the fall of 1947, an impressive group of freshman walk-ons matriculated to run for the Big Red. Two of them made the Olympic team in 1952, and others set numerous records and won a number of championships. It was a great way to bring Moakley's reign to a close.

He retired in 1949 and died six years later, but not before hearing of the successes of the athletes who had entered Cornell before he stepped down.

Lou Montgomery was hired as head coach in 1949 and stayed through 1965; he was followed by Jack Warner, who coached from 1968 to 1990, and then by Lou Duesing, who was head coach from 1990 to 2012. You might conclude that longevity is a prerequisite for great track coaches!

SIGMA NU

Sigma Nu fraternity has a proud and colorful history. Founded by three cadets at the Virginia Military Institute during a period of civil strife following the Civil War, Sigma Nu represented a radical departure from the times.

The system of physical abuse and hazing of underclassmen at VMI led two cadets to form the Legion of Honor, which soon became the Sigma Nu fraternity. Amid a back-drop of turmoil, North America's first "honor" fraternity was established.

When I arrived in the fall of 1947, I thought the Sigma Nu house was wonderful. It had an imposing front door, a spacious great hall, and a library and pool room that over-looked a grand dining room that had impressive chandeliers hanging from an eighteen-foot ceiling. There was also a room that featured photos of former Sigma Nu athletic greats—and that was just the first floor!

The next two floors were study rooms for the brothers. While each of these study rooms had a sleeping cot, most broth-ers, when not pulling an all-nighter, slept in a dormitory filled with double-decker cots and windows that were open all year round! The house had a majestic view of Cayuga Lake and the nearby gorges that rumbled between cavernous walls of stone.

Freshmen were rushed in the fall before they had a chance to get their bearings. It wasn't a great process, but at least you had to make up your mind rather quickly. My father and uncle were Sigma Nu brothers at Penn State; that was good enough for me, so I pledged the Gamma Theta Chapter of Sigma Nu.

In the fall of 1947, many brothers were returning from the service and were often as much as five years older than we lowly freshmen. The other distinguishing feature of Gamma Theta was that we were recognized as *the* jock house since the captains of the football, soccer, basketball, and polo teams were brothers.

Somehow, the honor principle on which Sigma Nu was

founded got lost in translation as there was a lot of hazing, just as there had been at Mercersburg, where we had to go through a paddle line before we could discard the black socks that were standard garb for all newbies.

However, the hazing "bar" was raised at Gamma Theta. We had to lie on our backs in the grand dining room with our mouths wide open so upperclassmen could drop raw eggs into them! We had to carve our own paddles, which were used when we were led blindfolded into the mystical and sacred Chapter Room, and asked, "How many fraternities are there at Cornell?" The answer was, of course, "Only one," but my paddle got significant use before I caught on!

LIFELONG FRIENDS AT CORNELL

My Sigma Nu pledge class of eighteen was terrific; many of them are still my best friends. Jack Vinson was my best man, my son Chuck's godfather, and my roommate for two years; we were both mechanical engineers. Stu Campbell, Sandy Beach, "Moose" Miller, and Buzz de Cordova have been regular reunion and golfing buddies. Some of my closest reunion friends are men I didn't know particularly well when we were students but now are dear friends, along with their wives.

ACADEMIC STRUGGLES AND ATHLETIC SUCCESS

As idyllic as Cornell is, I was in for a rude awakening academically. In my first term, I nearly flunked early exams in both chemistry and physics. So much for my cum laude preparation!

In the second term of my sophomore year (1949), I encountered further scholastic difficulty in a psychology class, which required Bob Kane (Cornell's director of athletics) to request that a professor represent me in front of the Petitions Committee.

In a letter on June 30, 1949 (after my NCAA and AAU wins), Kane scolded me in writing. "A fellow with your abilities should not let this happen again. It is not fair to yourself to get other than honor grades when you have the capacity to do so. In studying your academic record in connection with this probation case, I was quite amazed at your past record; and certainly this helped in presenting the petition in this instance."

Kane concluded his letter: "Hope you have a good summer. Get a lot of rest and eat a lot of fattening food so we'll have something to take off of you next year. Looking forward to seeing you in the fall. Please give my best to your Dad and Mother. Very best regards—PS: And work on your arms this summer!"

But there were academic successes, too. Professor Moynihan, my favorite teacher at Cornell, inspired me with his courses in metallurgy, which were much more interesting than those dealing with heat transfer! I did just fine in his courses, which set the stage for much of what I would do at Lenape Forge for the next twenty years. Eventually I would bounce back academically, juggling school, fraternity, marriage, and training for the Olympics.

MARRIAGE AND CHILDREN

Ithaca is a great place to live, learn, and develop. In my case, I had two separate living experiences at Cornell, one before and one after getting married. As a freshman, I lived with an upper-classman in one of the few permanent dormitories on campus; the next two years, I lived in my fraternity, which I loved.

On August 26, 1950, Nancy McAbee and I married, having already made arrangements to rent a basement apartment on Hanshaw Road in Cayuga Heights from Herb and Kay Ensworth, who became good friends. We loved living with them.

Our apartment felt smaller when our son, Charles III, arrived on November 13, 1951. While Nancy and I did enjoy chaperoning house parties at Sigma Nu, we spent what "leisure" time we had playing bridge with the Ensworths or with Coach Montgomery and his wife, who lived only a few blocks away on Highland Road.

A CORNELL MAN FOR LIFE

I didn't know it at the time, but Ithaca would end up providing two important bookends in my journey. The second bookend would come almost fifty years after I graduated.

But as July 21, 1952, approached, there were two constants in my life: pursuing my BME degree and running for Olympic gold. When my college eligibility ended after four years, I was on my own and began competing for the New York Athletic Club.

And after I graduated, my experience at Cornell continued to enhance my life in many other ways. In 1978 I was elected a charter member of Cornell's Athletic Hall of Fame; I was further honored to be chosen "athlete of the decade" for the 1950s by the *Cornell Daily Sun*, and just recently, I was voted the third most important Cornell athlete of all time in a survey run by *Cornell* magazine.

In 2000 I was elected to serve as a lifetime member of the Cornell Council and discovered that there is no gathering more stimulating than the annual joint trustee and council meeting each October.

I am not surprised that my greatest enrichment continues to come from the people of Cornell: faculty, administrators, fellow students, alumni, and friends.

I have always liked the way Romeyn Berry (class of 1904), a farmer, author, columnist, lawyer, and former graduate manager of the Cornell University Athletic Association, addressed the college experience.

It's probably a good thing for a student to take the problems of the world seriously so long as he is not permitted to take himself too seriously. And he can't do the latter in a university. They won't let him. The influences are all in the other direction. Universities are the hardiest of human organisms. Many of them have survived nations, changing forms of government, and all the new methods of warfare. They've learned through the centuries that the four undergraduate years constitute youth's little springtime, in which their students acquire the rudiments of culture, the tools of understanding, and along with them the ability to absorb beauty, song, laughter, friendship and group solidarity. It puts them in good company when they're alone, sweetens their youth, and when they're old permits them to hear bells, half-remembered songs, and the rustle of the ivy outside their study windows.

Let it always be so!

Chapter 6

BUILDING A FAMILY

To put the world in order, we must first put the nation in order;
to put the nation in order, we must first put the family in order;
to put the family in order, we must first cultivate our personal life;
we must first set our hearts right.

—CONFUCIUS

MY COPILOT

Judith and I were married on June 23, 1971, in Mary Dodd Brown Chapel on the campus of Lincoln University just outside Oxford, Pennsylvania. I was forty-two, Judith was twenty-eight. Our small family wedding was followed by a communion service in St. Christopher's Episcopal Church, where Judith had played the organ. It was for each of us a second marriage, and we already had seven children between us. The somewhat rotund priest hesitated when he reached the place

in the service where he was about to pray for "future proge-
ny." As he observed our children of various ages, sizes, and
hairstyles sitting in the first pew, his eyes twinkled, and he
asked, "Is this part really necessary?" This was a small family
gathering, but there would be no "small" anything from that
point forward!

QUALITY BONDS

My family has always meant everything to me. I'm indebted
to Judith for so much but particularly for helping me to understand that it's the quality of time spent with a child that
counts most, not the quantity. It's not easy to combine families! Our first Christmas in 1971 was classic: All seven children were gathered around the dining-room table with not
a lot in common except their respective parent's happiness.
While we were washing dishes that evening, Judith carefully
explained to me why my "quantity" approach to family time
was of little interest to this audience and why it would be a
very good idea if we spent New Year's Eve in New York City
at the opera. It took some time, but we are close to being one
family today.

How do you build strong bonds and mesh common interests within a family? It's more than love; I unconditionally
love each of my nine children the same. I focus on the unique
common interests I have with each one, and the bonding
sometimes takes us all by surprise. I'm a planner, but you
don't always get to pick your bonding times, and they don't
always go the way you think they should.

EVERY ONE A GEM

When Judith and I were married, our children ranged in age from nineteen to eight, and in many ways, they were very different from one another, some more in their formative years than others. Brian and Amanda were born in 1975 and 1977, and in a peculiar move mandated by the New York courts, I then adopted Judith's three children and they changed their last name to Moore. We now had a total of nine children— one big variegated family!

Chuck was probably the most gifted athlete (a baseball player and all-state Delaware soccer player); Jim ran cross-country at George School; David played number one on his Mercersburg squash team; Susan played field hockey for Mercersburg and the University of Arizona and competed at the Intermountain finals in Utah. Kevin and Chris played soccer, basketball, and golf in high school, and developed excellent singing voices as well as being good athletes. Along with assuming governance responsibilities in their respective churches, they both continue singing in their church choirs today. Brian played soccer and golf at Mercersburg and skied at Cornell. Margi and Amanda invested their leisure time in nonathletic school organizations and activities. Not a slacker in the group!

Eight of our nine children attended private schools, including the six who went to boarding schools, and while we have great respect for private education, our children were also well served by their respective public schools. Seven of our children earned undergraduate degrees and four earned master's degrees. Jim thrived on his Quaker education at George School; others struggled at times, but all of them treasure their academic journeys. Brian's five-year Cornell stint exactly overlapped with my athletic directorship there; that's like having your cake and eating it, too!

Our children's careers are as varied as their personalities. One spent three decades as a diplomat in the State Department, one spent more than twenty years on Wall Street, and others were in industrial sales, retail sales, information technology, wealth management, property management, fiber optics engineering, and interior design. They have all worked hard and been successful; I am enormously proud of every one of them.

They each have special talents, but most of them are quite competitive, which is always on display at our annual Family Mountain Challenge at Edgemoor, our Pennsylvania mountain home. The Sisters Three (Susan, Margi, and Amanda, with three more different personalities the world has never seen) can always be relied on for song, poetry, and laughter. Nothing is more meaningful than when the gang, at least those who can, gather around our piano to sing with Judith accompanying. I should also mention that Judith plays the piano, organ, and Irish harp. Hiking, reading, crossword puzzles, card playing, and storytelling are enjoyed by all, but golfing remains a "guy thing" for the most part.

Four of the children are married and have great wives. Jim and his partner, Richard, were married in 2013 near the end of their State Department tour. Sadly, the strain of divorce has not spared our family. In addition to Judith and me, three of our children have experienced four divorces. We all have learned from those experiences.

The good news is that we have sixteen grandchildren, whose ages range from thirty-seven to less than one. Our sixteenth grandchild was born in early January of 2017 (1/7/17 for the numerologists out there). While many of our family members are scattered around the country, we work at visiting them or arrange for them to come to Edgemoor. We celebrated Rio 2016 for the better part of two weeks at Edgemoor. We turned our house and several neighboring houses into Olympic villages. We ate and drank everything Brazilian as we streamed the Olympic competition from Rio. All nine children, twelve of our then-fifteen grandchildren, and eight spouses and significant others were in attendance. We were especially glad our oldest son, Chuck, could join us despite his battle with stage four melanoma. No better time could have been had by all, and we were grateful to be able to cherish all of our children before Chuck passed away on February 1, 2017.

ACROSS THE GLOBE

We celebrate birthdays, anniversaries, and, of course, the Olympic Games! While we are usually scattered to the four winds, in August we came together for a few days as a family unit, which included a sister, a brother-in-law, a niece and her family, and a couple of dogs. We shared personal history, love, respect, experiences, goals, ideas, and the skills required to overcome differences. We don't all share the same DNA, but when we come together, we listen, learn, and stretch our-

Photo by Richard Liebert

Judith and I with all nine children together for a special celebration at Laporte during the 2016 Summer Olympics.

selves to better understand what it means to be a part of this unwieldy far-flung family.

Travel has been a key component in educating and binding our family together. With various family members, we have attended the Summer Olympic Games in Munich, Montreal, Los Angeles, Barcelona, and Atlanta, as well as the Winter Games in Salt Lake City. With friends, Judith and I have also attended the Games in Sydney and London. Equally important, we have made a practice of visiting Jim and Richard wherever they end up—in Cairo, Karachi, Abu Dhabi, Madras, Buenos Aires, Quito, Ankara, Colombo, and Curaçao—often with two or more children in tow. We have taken our children and their partners to many foreign places and islands, including golf trips. Each child will tell you that these journeys were defining parts of their lives.

Judith and I have been fortunate to travel to all seven continents, including an amazing trip to Antarctica with Cornell's Adult University. Since 1973, we have shared much of our travel through photographic essays on our website (www.charlieandjudith.com). Because I did so much foreign traveling on business (taking Judith whenever possible or practical), I had to learn early on how best to get up to speed on the host country's cultural, political, and religious background. Engaging in my hosts' personal interests has been critical for me.

With our children now ranging in age from more than sixty to almost forty, I have zillions of treasured moments that fill me with pride. They include Santa's first visit to our home when the oldest, who was just beginning to question the existence of St. Nicholas, dove under a chair and never asked the question again. (Author's note: I'm still a believer.) I fondly remember pulling a sled with another son through six feet of snow to my parents to deliver Christmas dinner; this was the same child who asked me my toughest-ever question, "Dad, don't you ever take time to do nothing?" One son was an enterprising early riser who got a job at the age of ten and got on his school bus from work; it's no surprise that this same kid set the record for the most job offers coming out of business school. After Susan's first summer program at the Cornell Biological Field Station at Shackelton Point, she became the family expert in birding. When we were on a hiking trip in Arizona's Chiricahua Mountains, we unexpectedly came upon a large number of coatimundi (rare monkeylike creatures from South and Central America).

I've had the thrill of playing golf with the twins in Scotland and Ireland, with Brian in Scotland, and in father-son golf tournaments with David, Brian, and the twins at Pine Valley and Blind Brook. And I was thrilled to watch Chris and his family take a "lost boy" from Sudan into their home, help him complete his education, and be instrumental in founding with him the successful group Water for South Sudan, a well-drilling operation that provides clean water all across the country. I'm proud to have a daughter who has invented new ways to enjoy birthdays and do the hokey pokey. And *no*, that's *not* what it's all about! I was happy to have a son to learn to fly-fish with and then do that with him in the wilds of Alaska. And I love having a daughter who writes me sensitive poetry. She's been my partner in so many ways, including riding together on top of an elephant in Nepal while we hunted for tigers! And throughout my life's journey with this group of nine, a common love has been enjoying what we call "fun facts." At mealtime, we each share our personal discoveries and impressions for the day. In this way, we share our love and excitement for the planet and one another.

So that's nine children born across twenty-six years who now function as a closely connected, mostly happy family. I suppose that our rewards and challenges could fill several books. However, the process of building this family has been the greatest gift and opportunity I could ever have.

I am honored to be the "patriarch."

Chapter 7

CORPORATE TURNAROUNDS

Your life does not get better by chance, it gets better by change.

—JIM ROHN

LEARNING ON THE GO!

After more than two decades at Lenape Forge, I needed to move on to new management challenges and new business experiences. Judith and I had been married for two years by 1973. Wouldn't finding a new community for a new family make sense?

When I was offered the job of running Interpace Corporation's recently acquired porcelain insulator business in LeRoy, New York, Judith and I were ready, or at least we thought we were! It was a risk; I had never worked anyplace else or with anything other than steel forgings. And it was difficult to uproot our family and sell our wonderful one-hundred-acre farm that we had recently purchased.

We didn't know it then, but we were about to start nearly twenty years of running companies in need of change and uprooting our family several times along the way. Each of my five major career moves involved entirely different markets, categories, products, underlying technology, and global cultures. But the three manufacturing companies were distressed businesses with stockholders who wanted to see value created.

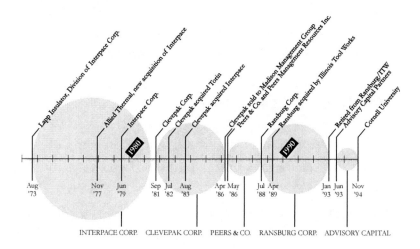

It's fairly common today to play career "hopscotch" as a way of self-development or simply staying afloat. It was far less comforting in the troubled '70s. But I've always been drawn to transitions. Talk about risk, navigating change, and going for it!

Time is definitely not on your side when you need to turn around a company. The challenge is to determine whether the content of the business or your leadership/organizational role gets priority attention. Both are extremely important, of course, but the first six months on the job are the most critical. After that, you own all of the present and future problems!

It was this tapestry of experiences that shaped my broader perspectives on how corporate strategies can respond and benefit from outside pressure. It was in this go-go period of turnarounds that I gained an invaluable education in acquisitions, governance, and banking. As I wrestled with the nuances of these fundamental levers of organizational change, I was exposed to brilliant mentors, some very innovative products, and a world of new opportunities to serve customers, employees, stockholders, and communities.

INTERPACE CORPORATION

Interpace grew out of the Lock Joint Pipe Company and was focused on ceramic materials. I joined the Lapp Insulator Division in LeRoy, New York, in August 1973 as vice president and general manager. A year later I was named president, and Interpace was reorganized into four divisions: Concrete Pipe (the largest producer of prestressed concrete cylinder pipe), Heavy Clay and Minerals (refractories, clay pipe, salt, etc.), Retail and Commercial Products (retail and commercial dinnerware and architectural tile), and my Lapp Insulator Division, which also included Ceramaseal (ceramic seals) and PULSAfeeder (metering pumps). Turns out I had left a high-flying conglomerate only to join a miniconglomerate.

Bill Hartman from ITT's Grinnell Corp. joined Interpace as CEO in 1974 and was determined to develop Interpace into a dynamic residential and commercial construction business. He was a demanding boss who principally focused on financial results, as he had done successfully at ITT.

A FAST COURSE IN THE ELECTRIC UTILITY INDUSTRY

The electric utility industry is capital intensive and cyclical. Interpace acquired Lapp at the top of a market cycle that was on its way down, which caused them to rethink management personnel. Brent Mills had served as president until the acquisition, at which point he retired but joined the Interpace board. Ralph Ganiard took over but was moved to manufacturing, his area of expertise.

I came to Lapp without having a clue about what a dielectric was or that insulators had dual mechanical and electrical functions. But what I did learn in a hurry was that Lapp had the best design engineers, the best process and quality engineers, and that their "porcelain makeability" had no peer, all qualities that were prized in the utility marketplace. Our customers were utilities of all sizes and original equipment manufacturers that used our insulators in the equipment they manufactured for utilities.

A NEW PHASE FOR LAPP

A reenergized Lapp, I believed, had to lead in its market with high-margin products that delivered solutions for customers. We were very fortunate to attract talented people to the team.

We brought on board an international sales manager and a vice president and director of technology; and we expanded and reinforced our sales representatives. We relocated our PULSAfeeder operation, introduced new products, and hired a new general manager.

We continued to strengthen management in all areas: manufacturing, process control, product engineering, personnel administration and controllership, and promoted two existing members of the management team, Gene Watson and Dick Hampel, to assistant general manager positions. We set records in safety and for lowering absenteeism, as well as reigniting our local division communications. We created a public relations campaign that included a town hall meeting in the LeRoy High School that celebrated the theme Let's All Push Priorities. Incidentally, our community engagement included arranging for sections of the Rochester Philharmonic Orchestra to perform and work with the local schools.

We also set division records in sales and earnings in 1975, but with the utility market in the tank, new orders were low and projected to drop even lower. New products and cost efficiencies were enough to mitigate the industry trough, and we were helped by the strong growth in PULSAfeeder's and Ceramaseal's profits, where margins were twice as high.

LEAVING LAPP TO HEAD UP ALLIED THERMAL

Real progress continued on all fronts through 1976 and 1977. On November 28, 1977, Bill Hartman announced that

I would assume responsibility as liaison executive for Allied Thermal Corp. of New Britain, Connecticut, reporting directly to Hartman. The announcement went on to say that Interpace was acquiring Allied Thermal, which provided the building and construction industry with components for ventilating and air-conditioning equipment. What the announcement kindly avoided saying was that the new "executive in charge" knew no more about HVAC equipment than he had known about utility insulators back in August 1973! I faced another steep learning curve.

Leaving an entity where you have made such a difference as I did at Lapp is never easy; it had been fun and we liked our lives in western New York. In hindsight, I think giving priority to my leadership/organization role proved very beneficial for this turnaround. Most satisfying was the fact that the management team I had recruited over four and a half years was fully qualified to carry on and build the enterprise.

VALUE CREATION AT ALLIED THERMAL

Allied Thermal Corporation had been principally formed out of two companies in the HVAC business: Tuttle & Bailey and Hart & Cooley. I was to be appointed president and CEO of Allied Thermal as soon as the acquisition closed. It had been a difficult acquisition for Bill Hartman as there had been a bidding war with the Jim Walter Corporation, and there was speculation that Interpace had paid too much for its HVAC prize.

My job was to see precisely what we had bought and how we could create value with this new turnaround. Hart

& Cooley manufactured a complete line of grilles, registers, and diffusers that were primarily sold to the residential market, as well as producing a line of Type-B vents for gas-fired appliances and all-fuel systems. Tuttle & Bailey's register and grille line was designed for commercial applications, and they manufactured an extensive range of fans, including whole-house attic fans.

And Tuttle & Bailey had something that I had had no experience with—an office union. There were also other plants in the U.S., Canada, Brazil, Australia, and Europe. My job, it turned out, was to rationalize products and markets, take a hard look at management, address the office union situation, improve morale and efficiency, and figure out how to create sustainable value. In the meantime, I did a lot of shuttling between outlying plants, my favorite being the Hart & Cooley operation located in the town of Holland, Michigan, just off Lake Michigan, which is also known as the tulip center of the United States.

New Britain was settled as early as 1682. It became known as the Hardware City because the Stanley Works, now known as Stanley/Black & Decker, started there. The city, with a population of more than 70,000, one-quarter of which were of Polish extraction, was dark, dirty, and very industrial in this era before quality emission controls. Our offices were particularly drab; nonetheless, we held an Interpace board meeting there, where I was elected senior vice president for building products and a director of Interpace. Bill Hartman then asked me to accept new responsibilities, and after only a year, he asked me to relocate to Parsippany, New Jersey, the corporate headquarters. Another move!

When we had moved from LeRoy, we had been advised by friends to live in West Hartford, where we had purchased a lovely Tudor-style house. We loved the house, the neighborhood, and the people. Judith had just finished remodeling our kitchen, and the flower gardens were at their peak when I announced we were moving to New Jersey! I was prepared for her to throw in the towel on this "turnaround stuff"; even the wonderful couple, Norbert and Eleanor Gale, who had moved from LeRoy to help take care of Brian and Amanda, were not prepared to follow us to New Jersey. After a short time helping us settle in New Jersey, they retired to Florida. Nonetheless, we moved to a lovely rambling old house on Kitchell Road in Convent Station, New Jersey (near Morristown), on June 25, 1979.

MOVING UP IN THE RANKS

It was different working in the corporate headquarters: spacious hallways and paneled offices, fine paintings and sculpture, special garage parking and, the ultimate, a helicopter pad beside a lovely lake. What's not to like? I was used to walking into an adjoining plant and talking with operating people. That was still my job, but now I was closer to Manhattan than any of the manufacturing facilities.

By now, the Hartman strategy for creating a strong building products portfolio had produced a miniconglomerate that included Lapp, Hart & Cooley, Tuttle & Bailey, Mansfield (sanitary ware), Chemineer (waste-product devices), and Ward Manufacturing (a cast-iron fitting and nipple business).

I had firsthand knowledge of Lapp and Allied Thermal, and Interpace had only recently acquired Chemineer and Mansfield. And I had personally hounded Charlie Ward for a year or so to buy his family's business located in Blossburg, Pennsylvania. Bill Hartman knew this foundry from his Grinnell days; and we finally got it, and I was able to attract an outstanding general manager.

In the meantime, interest rates were soaring, and Bill Hartman began divesting $70 million in assets at book value. By the middle of 1981, 75 percent of Interpace's original assets had been divested, including its core division, Lock Joint Products. With this divestiture, Interpace was the same size as when Bill Hartman took it over. Would the economy recover? Would Interpace consider going private?

GETTING HIRED IS MUCH MORE FUN
THAN GETTING FIRED

During this time, we had several exploratory meetings with the investment firm KKR, and they were not encouraging. And two senior executives recruited by Hartman were leaving Interpace. I both respected and liked Bill, but he was demanding and could be difficult. He expected a lot and did not tolerate substandard performance. John Maypole joined Interpace in 1966 and was the second-ranking officer as executive vice president and director. Earlier in the year, I had been promoted to executive VP, COO, and director.

On May 11, 1981, Bill called me into his office, and said, "Charlie, we have more horsepower than we need; I am going to let you go." There it was; I had been fired! But I agreed with Hartman's assessment that we were talent heavy at the top. The next day I met with the board, and at lunch afterward, I got all kinds of congratulations and good advice, but it was not quite as much fun as standing on a podium with a gold medal around my neck!

Interpace was extremely fair in terms of compensation and outplacement, which I jumped right into at Fuchs, Cuthrell & Company. Here I was at age fifty-two learning how to market myself, rewriting a résumé, crafting an "elevator speech," practicing in front of a TV screen, and working with a counselor on "gotcha" questions. The process worked, and I was eager to get back to work. It didn't take long!

On September 2, 1981, it was announced that I had been elected president, CEO, and a member of the board of directors of Clevepak Corporation.

CLEVEPAK CORPORATION:
THE PAPER/PACKAGING COMPANY

Bill Green and Edgar Bronfman were the sole stockholders when they acquired Cleveland Container Corporation and its eleven facilities for $2.5 million in 1962.

The company, financially troubled and located in Cleveland, Ohio, manufactured composite cans, cores, abrasives, and containers for artillery shells and hand grenades. Bill Green was determined to make his new acquisition work.

The next year, Green hired Hubert McPherson as president and COO. He was brought in to address lax management practices and would serve as the company's hands-on manager for the next dozen years and would return in 1981 to assume day-to-day management until I arrived.

In those twenty years, enormous changes took place: acquisitions (some worked, others did not), divestitures, diversification (some worked, some did not). Under Green's and McPherson's management, the company posted rising profits for thirteen consecutive years and split the stock one hundred for one. They also purchased two paper mills and a manufacturer of braided cords with metal and plastic attachments that were used in specialty packaging.

In 1975 Clevepak relocated corporate management and some divisional staff to White Plains, New York, in an effort to improve and streamline overall operations. On October 4, 1976, Green watched proudly as Clevepak took its place alongside 1,570 other companies on the NYSE.

At the time, rising energy prices and a declining demand for paperboard began threatening to reverse Clevepak's fortunes, but despite a frustrating economy, Clevepak continued to acquire companies.

Sadly, Bill Green died on January 22, 1979, at the age of sixty-three; his wife, the author Judith H. Green, became a director, and Edgar Bronfman returned to take up his old friend's duties as chairman of the board.

Net income recovered in 1980, ending three years of decline. In the meantime, the current CEO who had replaced McPherson when he had stepped down in 1975 left, and McPherson returned to Clevepak to find a new CEO. "Mac" was fully in charge of the recruitment process and was a godsend for me once the board approved my appointment. However, I won't ever forget my initial interview with Bronfman. I was ushered into his spacious art-filled office in the Seagram Building at 375 Park Avenue, and I couldn't take my eyes off an amazing Rodin sculpture standing proudly in the center of the room! In my interview, he was extremely friendly, but after encouraging me to take the job, he concluded our talk by saying, "One thing, Charlie, don't ever embarrass me."

A ROCKY START

So what had I gotten myself into? Clevepak had modest manufacturing facilities all over the country that produced and sold solid fiberboard partitions (to separate glass bottles in cartons), folding cartons (to hold pizzas, etc.), cardboard containers (for Kraft's grated cheese, for example), cardboard cores (originally for military applications and now for commercial and consumer products), flexible hosing for carburetor air ducts (at one time controlling 85 percent of the domestic car market), specialized pollution-control equipment, and a host of wastepaper collection and processing centers. We had twenty-six facilities including two paper mills, one on the banks of the Hudson River and the other in Eaton, Indiana.

With the exception of the braided cords and air ducts, the rest of the business was very low margin with no competitive differentiation. The two paper mills were ticking time bombs for environmental fines. There was little cohesion in management and sales practices across the company. Why?

Because they were acquired and then were permitted to operate as separate entrepreneurial entities.

The debt was manageable but difficult partly because Green's widow, who owned roughly 35 percent of the stock, depended on her dividend. The short answer was that Clevepak could not be expected to sustain earnings in excess of its dividend obligation.

THE HARD TRUTH

I first went to McPherson, who knew more than anybody about the past and the future of Clevepak. I also went to the general managers of the plants to better understand their challenges, and I sought the counsel of my administrative staff and also relied on the advice of John Haigney and Peter Rado.

I then went to Bronfman and Green to share what I had learned in my first six months. This was not going to be easy, but I was prepared. In the special board meeting called to review my findings, I was quite clear: I saw no way to create sustainable value with the existing assets, and therefore I was recommending the orderly sale of *all* corporate assets. The only option I could suggest was to replace them with new businesses that could create value in excess of our dividend obligation.

There was not a lot of discussion for such a serious matter. All six directors wanted to continue the corporate entity of Clevepak and were willing to trust me in this challenging asset turnover. It was quite a vote of confidence—tinged with desperation on their part!

SELLING CLEVEPAK'S ASSETS

With great help from McPherson, who knew the main paper-board players, we started at once. We sold our partition operations to Sonoco, the dominant company in the field. We sold our regional carton, core, container, and wastepaper-collection facilities mostly on a one-off basis at or around book value.

During this time, I kept in close touch with my directors. On a quarterly basis, Edgar would invite me to lunch in his private corporate dining room; what a culinary treat that was, although we agreed on very little: certainly not politics, religion, or women.

A NEW PERSONAL PHASE

After much searching for a new home and weighing the merits of Connecticut versus New York, we purchased a very cozy, comfortable house on Lake Avenue in Greenwich, Connecticut, a decision we never regretted despite the "asset uncertainty" at Clevepak.

It was around this time that McPherson casually told me that Clevepak had leased a one-bedroom apartment for him in the Essex House on Central Park South and now that he would be coming east only for board meetings, he hoped that Judith and I would make some use of it! Well, of course, I said, "Yes, sir." It was a terrific space that overlooked the park, and I made great use of it for business, and Judith and I loved it for all that is great about Manhattan: Lincoln Center, Carnegie Hall, Fifth Avenue—which were all on our doorstep!

SETTING OUR SIGHTS ON
TORIN CORPORATION

Tappani Seppa, whom I had installed as general manager of PULSAfeeder in Rochester while I was still at Lapp, joined me as strategy director at Clevepak. We had identified Torin Corporation, a highly respected leading manufacturer of air-moving equipment and wire-forming machinery with fourteen plants, 1,600 employees, and revenues in 1981 of $92 million as a potential acquisition.

But they weren't for sale. They were headquartered in Torrington, Connecticut, where I had visited a number of times. One day Tappani suggested that Clevepak purchase some Torin shares to let them know we were interested. We also engaged Lehman Brothers to assist us in bringing more pressure. Whatever we did worked, and Torin agreed to be acquired for $25.6 million, with the deal closing in July 1982.

This happened to be one of Dan Doctoroff's first deals at Lehman Brothers, and the beginning of a new and exciting friendship for me. By coincidence, Dan would go on to run New York City's strong bid to host the 2012 Summer Olympics. (I was the chair of the USOC's bid city task force that selected New York as our candidate.) This was followed by Dan's serving as Mayor Michael Bloomberg's deputy mayor of development, the CEO of Bloomberg LP, and a member of CECP's board of directors. Dan and his wife, Alisa, continue to be our good friends.

A NEW ERA FOR CLEVEPAK AND TORIN

As we embarked on a new era for a "redirected" Clevepak, I had a lot to do: integrating Torin, divesting the remaining paperboard and specialty packaging units, and implementing cost controls to reshape Clevepak into a newly balanced, high-performance company.

Torin was comprised of seven domestic and seven international plants. I was traveling constantly to meet new managers and staff, and conduct operation reviews. Our board of directors was expanded to include Gerry Cahill (the Torin president), Rufus Stillman (the former Torin chairman), and Keith Cunningham, a former executive partner and vice chair of the accounting firm Touche Ross and Co.

CELEBRATING CLEVEPAK'S TWENTIETH

We chose to celebrate Clevepak's twentieth anniversary and welcome Torin and our new directors with a gala dinner on September 7, 1982, at the Carlyle Hotel in New York.

A special song to the tune of "Lullaby of Broadway" was written and lustily sung; an elegant cake featuring replicas of the leading brands our partitions protected (Seagram's VO, Heinz ketchup, Kraft mayonnaise, and General Foods' Maxwell House coffee) was baked and fancifully iced; and a limited edition of a colored intaglio by Rochester artist Jack Matott that incorporated our company logo was commissioned and given to guests to herald a new era.

Judith and I hosting the Clevepak-Torin dinner at the Carlyle Hotel celebrating Clevepak's twentieth anniversary in 1982.

GETTING THE BALL ROLLING

Torin was a good start in our diversifying into industrial and engineering products, but Tappani Seppa and I were looking

for additional opportunities. On April 6, 1983, Interpace announced a management buyout for $132 million. The year
after I had left, Interpace reported a loss of $2.7 million after
earning a profit of $8.8 million the previous year on only 5
percent lower revenues. Earlier in the year, Harold C. Simmons and others had taken a 9 percent investment position in
the company, which likely motivated the management group
to take action. Seppa and I had the advantage of knowing
the Interpace businesses very well, and we wondered if we
should put together a team to explore our investment opportunities. The company was clearly "in play" because we knew
the Interpace board had retained Dillon, Read & Company to
advise them, but the shareholders would be required to vote
on management's bid.

With our Clevepak board's encouragement, we decided
to approach Dillon, Read to offer close to book value or $33
a share (management's offer was $30 for each of Interpace's
4 million common shares, plus another nearly $12 million for
the company's 5 percent convertible preferred).

On May 7, 1983, trading of Interpace stock was halted as reports circulated of a new offer; the stock was up to
thirty-one and one-quarter, up one-quarter when trading was
halted at eleven a.m. and the two offers were disclosed. One
was made by the group that included the company's top management, which would take the company private. The other
offer was ours. The announcement of the offers also referred
to Simmons's earlier interest and the fact that arbitrager Ivan
Boesky had taken a 6 percent position in Interpace common
stock. Boesky commented that "Interpace is an undervalued

company." The fat was now in the fire, and we had a lot to do to complete our due diligence and secure financing, being advised by Lehman Brothers and Skadden Arps Slate Meagher & Flom LLP.

THE PHONE CALL I NEVER FORGOT

May 3, 1983, was a day I won't forget. I was meeting with the Interpace board of directors (without the executives leading the buyout) when someone insisted that I take a phone call at the table. It was that phone call from Judith saying that my father had just suffered a fatal heart attack on a golf course in Fort Myers, Florida.

I turned to the Interpace directors, all of whom I knew as I had been one of them just two years earlier; told them what had happened; asked for their indulgence; and requested a grace period of several weeks that they readily granted. I left the room.

MERGING CLEVEPAK AND INTERPACE

After Dad's funeral and my attending to some time-sensitive items as his executor, I launched back into negotiating with a consortium of banks and securing the assets of both Interpace and Clevepak.

As I look back on that experience, there was little time to address operations, cost controls, and product development, let alone customers or family! I was completely engaged in selling the banks and the Interpace board of directors on the value to be created by merging the two companies, and I was fortunate to have the complete support of my Clevepak board throughout the challenging process.

I have no idea how the Interpace board decided which offer to accept. Everyone knew I had the advantage of knowing both companies, their products, customers, and management teams. But I still needed to secure the financing, and I was suddenly learning how difficult that would be. Finally, the Interpace board accepted Clevepak's sweetened offer of $35 a share, the financing terms were negotiated, and our June tender offer brought in 81.4 percent of Interpace's stock. This was announced on August 16, 1983, as the first part of a two-step transaction, with the second step being an exchange of two new shares of Clevepak preferred stock for each remaining Interpace share. Whew!

INTEGRATING THE COMPANIES

But the acceptance of our offer was just the beginning. Interpace had management contracts to address, and I was very pleased when COO John Maypole, general counsel Hal Sanford, and several other officers of Interpace agreed to join Clevepak, at least for an interim period. They knew a lot more than I did about "where the bodies were buried," especially some old liabilities and other divestiture issues, all of which our acquisition documents had done as much as possible to avoid.

In addition to covering operations, there were a host of management issues and unfinished bank covenants to address. But I felt very good about adding two Interpace directors to our Clevepak board: M. Kathryn Eickhoff (EVP of Townsend-Greenspan and associate director of economics for OMB) and Bob Lear (former chair/CEO of F. M. Schaefer Corporation and founder of the Executive-in-Residence program at Columbia Business School). We also added Paul Boylan, Esq., of LeRoy, New York, who was very influential in encouraging the 20 percent of Interpace stockholders (as part of the Lapp acquisition) to vote for our tender offer.

NEW DIGS FOR A NEW ERA

We had grown out of our White Plains office, so when we learned that a developer was building another office complex not far away, we leased an entire floor at 2500 Westchester Avenue when it was still just girders and concrete. We had what we considered to be a creatively arranged space, convenience, and a spectacular view of Long Island Sound.

We also had some good pieces of American sculpture and a lot of prints and drawings that were mostly in storage. By then, we had already sold some of Torin's Marcel Breuer buildings and the Parsippany headquarters to reduce the debt created by the Interpace acquisition. We did not sell the Torin art collection, which we relocated to our new offices, thereby enhancing our workplace and furthering our reputation as a caring corporate entity. We moved into our sparkling new offices in May 1984.

THE END OF THE ROAD FOR CLEVEPAK

In February 1985, we sold our Lapp Insulator unit for $32 million to Jefferson Management, a subsidiary of Great American Management and Investment. Still struggling with our debt, we were surprised in July by what we believed to be an attractive and credible offer for the rest of the company from Andlinger & Company, a private investment banking and management company organized to acquire manufacturing companies. Unfortunately, we were unable to agree on terms for a definitive agreement.

The negotiations were abandoned, but now our company was in play! Finally, after exhausting all avenues, we sold what remained of Clevepak to the Madison Management Group (80 percent owned by GAMI) in a transaction valued at $97 million, which was announced on October 23, 1985, and closed on April 2, 1986.

REFLECTIONS ON INVESTMENTS AND DIVESTMENTS

Were shareholders well served in all of this buying and selling? That, of course, depends on when they bought or sold their stocks. It was a grueling experience for those who worked so hard to make it work. We never had the time to consolidate and improve the product lines; the same can be said about management. Melding three different cultures and managements into a cohesive team to manage a larger company would take more time than we had. By late 1984, our markets had faltered, particularly for our more cyclical products. There is no forgiveness in bank covenants and payment schedules, nor should there be. But that is what drove us instead of real value creation.

A TURNING POINT AND NEW LEAPS

It had been a crazy twelve years for me. But I couldn't help but think: What next? I thanked everyone who helped along the way whether or not they were pleased with the results or the disruptions. I tried to learn from the successes and mistakes. I accepted all the blame; the buck did stop with me. I needed to regroup and move on! So I did.

But to what? With my most recent "asset scramble" experience—mergers, acquisitions, divestitures, and reorganizations—why not come at it from the other end, the investment or merchant banking end?

I thought I could identify acquisitions and/or divestitures for the many CEOs I knew if I ran an advisory or consulting service. I soon found out that it was necessary to spend 60 percent of my time developing new business, 40 percent servicing the business I had, and 20 percent administering my own business, which stretched even my normal workaholic day!

WOOED BY A BOUTIQUE FIRM

In mid-1986 I met Paul K. Kelly, the cofounder of Peers & Co., an international investment banking firm, where he served as president and CEO.

The principal investor in Peers was the Long-Term Credit Bank of Japan. After some discussion, Paul encouraged me to join his boutique firm as managing director and, taking advantage of my operating experience, to also serve as CEO of Peers Management Resources, a management consulting firm. I accepted on the provision that I could continue my "merchant banking" efforts on my own. And for the first time in my life, I started to commute daily by train, Greenwich to Manhattan.

I resigned from Peers in July 1988; and Kelly sold his equity interest in the firm to Kemper Corporation in 1990.

MERCHANT BANKING:
THE FIRST APPROACH

In my own merchant banking pursuits, I looked for a small business I could acquire or business units that I could serve as a middleman or sales agent for.

In the first instance, I called on Hank McKinnell, who was then Pfizer's strategy director and would later become chairman and CEO, to explore purchasing their nonstrategic refractories business. I also combined efforts with Carl Singer, chairman and founder of Fundamental Management, who specialized in troubleshooting, identifying problems associated with business management, and restoring financial stability to business organizations.

Carl and I met when we were unsuccessfully chasing a Boston-based instruments company; following that, I became an investor in and director of Fundamental, and served on several boards of the companies that we had taken an "active" investment position in.

THE FRUITFUL APPROACH

In another approach that bore fruit, I met with Chuck Hugel, CEO of Combustion Engineering, shortly after they had relocated their corporate headquarters from New York to Stamford, Connecticut. Over the years, Combustion had strayed from their core business of utility steam supply and were now trying to rationalize more than thirty-six companies that were divided into five or six business groups.

I was particularly interested in their C-E Natco business—a leader in oil and gas separation in the oil field services sector, and shared this opportunity with Pug Winokur, a Greenwich friend and former executive with Penn Central and then founder and CEO of Capricorn Management. Winokur purchased C-E Natco, and I was rewarded with a handsome finder's fee.

MORE TURNAROUNDS

Timing is everything! At exactly the right moment, Heidrick & Struggles came calling again. Was I interested in another turnaround that the financial "sharks" were already circling around? We would need to move from Greenwich, which we had loved for seven years, to Indianapolis. Another turnaround decision!

On July 25, 1988, I joined Ransburg Corporation as

president and chief executive officer. Their chairman/CEO had resigned under pressure in January and a director, Craig Smith, agreed to serve as interim CEO and lead the search committee. This would prove to be my ultimate turnaround challenge: a company rich in innovation that was shattered financially and demoralized—and a takeover target. Welcome to Indianapolis!

RANSBURG CORPORATION

My first goal was to understand the history of the company and its unique technology, which proved fascinating.

Harold Ransburg, the son of Harper Ransburg who was blind in one eye due to a plant accident, stumbled into inventing electrostatic spray painting because he detested cleaning his father's paint booth and hated to see his father lose hundreds of gallons of enamel due to an inefficient spraying process. His goal? To electrically charge the paint while spraying it on a grounded object, which caused the paint to collect on the item's surface. He applied for a patent in 1939. Then he eliminated the compressed air and atomized the paint with just electricity, thereby improving the process. However, it would take seven more years to develop this process.

After Ransburg built a new 80,000-square-foot facility in Indianapolis in 1958, a series of lawsuits and countersuits were filed over the misuse of patents, violations of antitrust laws, and unfair competition. Ransburg won these lawsuits that established important precedents for its patents.

The business grew internationally by leaps and bounds—even in Japan, where the company had to form a joint venture to satisfy the powerful Ministry of International Trade and Industry and pursue patent infringements.

In 1962 Harold had the opportunity to purchase the company and buy out his father and brothers; and Ransburg continued to enjoy success in the courtroom, including a major victory over Ford. The company went public in 1967.

By then, the whole finishing business was changing rapidly; it was going from hand spraying to automatic spraying. New powder coatings and water-based materials were being developed. Heightened environmental awareness was putting more pressure on manufacturers to reduce vapor emissions from their facilities. Liquid coatings contributed to this problem while powder posed few risks. By the end of 1973, Ransburg, with revenues of $44 million and 800 employees, led the world in the production of electrostatic painting equipment.

Don Kacek was made CEO in 1977 and chairman the following year when Harold Ransburg resigned that position. The Kacek strategy, which the board supported, was to concentrate on the industrial-equipment market and acquire companies that "faced little or no competition and integrate them into a powerful, profitable consortium."

Kacek was convinced that the 1980s were the decade of robotics, and his board agreed. Ransburg sent representatives around the world to find companies interested in developing a robotic alliance. In early 1980 they met with a subsidiary of Renault of France that was working on robotics for two specific areas: paint application and the welding of automotive bodies.

The match seemed ideal, and in October Ransburg announced an agreement, called Cybotech, between the two companies to develop, sell, and service advanced industrial robots, and located it in Indianapolis.

Cybotech put Ransburg in the national spotlight; the stock reached an all-time high of $37.80 per share in the second quarter of 1981.

In April 1982 Ransburg acquired GEMA AG in Switzerland, one of their best strategic purchases as it gave them a foothold in the North American powder-coating market.

However, capital equipment expenditures in the U.S. were falling to the lowest levels since WWII, and the demand for Cybotech robots increased only moderately while start-up costs for the project spiked.

In 1984 Ransburg lost money for the first time in its history. Internal management concluded that "electrostatic painting equipment and welding control equipment were not as universally applicable to robots as they had thought."

The board began to have serious doubts about Kacek's long-term strategy and cut the dividend on two occasions. They also approved a plan to divest most of Kacek's acquisitions including Cybotech, which had cost the company $28 million over an eight-year period.

By the end of 1987, Ransburg had lost almost $16 million. The board called an emergency meeting and decided that they had to make a management change. Kacek resigned as chairman, president, and CEO in January 1988. Craig Smith was then appointed interim CEO, and the rest is my story!

Smith, like McPherson at Clevepak, was terrific. He was completely forthcoming about the past although he had been a director only since 1979. He was equally candid with me about Ransburg being a takeover target. Tom Binford, later a close friend who was the longest serving Ransburg director, was extremely supportive. Once I accepted their offer, I was anxious to get into the fray.

STARTING OUR LIFE IN INDIANAPOLIS

We purchased a spiffy modern house (for us, at least) in Carmel, a suburb north of Indianapolis, and enrolled Brian, age fourteen, and Amanda, age twelve, in Park Tudor, an excellent private day school. We purposely made the journey by car from Greenwich to Indianapolis in order to acclimate ourselves to our new "flatland" home. We got another look at the lay of land when I surprised the family the next night with a helicopter ride over Indianapolis to celebrate Judith's birthday.

Relocation is tough! However, we soon attended the Indiana State Fair and took in a demolition derby; we were into it! Judith had already been invited to visit the Indianapolis Museum of Art, where she would soon become a board member. Adding to our good fortune, our home in Greenwich sold at a good price, which eventually gave us the means to build a swimming pool (our first and only) and relandscape our new property.

By September, I had been to St. Gallen, a town outside

of Zurich, to inspect our small well-managed GEMA operation there. I had also received my first phone call from one of those "sharks," LFC Financial. That was followed by an expression of interest by Eagle Industries, which was controlled by Sam Zell of Chicago.

THE CIRCLING SHARKS

This gets complicated! Great American Management and Investment, Inc., was incorporated in 1979. Sam Zell was the driving force, starting with only a 3.5 percent stake in GAMI with his primary interest being the $110-million tax-loss carry forwards. In February 1985 GAMI acquired Lapp Insulator, which turned out to be the start of a buying spree.

On April 2, 1986, GAMI acquired the remaining operations of Clevepak, whereupon they established a new industrial products subsidiary called Eagle Industries that became the parent company of eight operating units that I was very familiar with, including Lapp Insulator, Hart & Cooley, PULSAfeeder, and Ceramaseal. To pare down some debt, they sold PULSAfeeder in 1990. So here I was, face to face with Sam Zell again!

A WHITE KNIGHT SAVES THE DAY

While Indiana laws on takeovers are much more lenient than in many states, I still needed to move quickly. My board wanted the company to remain independent and I needed a "white knight" as backup. I had been introduced to John

Nichols, the chairman and CEO of Illinois Tool Works, a respected and diversified worldwide manufacturer of highly engineered components and industrial systems that was based in Chicago. John had joined ITW in 1980 and had been named president and CEO in 1981 and chairman in 1986. With my "months" of Ransburg experience, I described to him the background and potential of my company. John was intrigued, but despite all the acquisitions ITW had made, he had never done a "public deal" nor did he want to.

I convinced Nichols that Ransburg would add a compatible "third leg" to ITW's portfolio and that I would take every step to keep ITW out of the limelight and a bidding war. I also had to convince my board that remaining independent was not possible and that ITW would respect Ransburg's autonomy while playing a key role in returning us to profitability.

We got lucky with our white knight. As both Nichols and Zell resided in Chicago, Nichols had met the flamboyant investor and, in fact, had been nearly run off an Alpine ski slope the year before by Zell, who insisted on skiing faster than anyone else. It's fair to say that for several reasons there was little rapport between them!

While Eagle Industries bid $22.50 against ITW's $21.00, they dropped their bid after further reviewing Ransburg's information on March 10, and we signed a purchase agreement with ITW for about $170 million on April 1, 1989. Pretty quick work! One chapter of Ransburg's history was over. The company and its founder, Harold Ransburg, had revolutionized the finishing industry. Yes, the company had temporarily lost its way, and I was not able to maintain the company's independence. However, Ransburg had joined a great company that would grant it autonomy. It was time to get moving and traveling!

FREQUENT FLYER TO TOKYO

In no time, I was spending one week out of seven in Japan; that's a lot of time in Japan whether you like sushi or not, and I didn't at the time! My normal routine was to fly from Indianapolis to Minneapolis to Tokyo via Pan Am or Air Japan, ride the bullet train from Narita to my hotel in Tokyo, walk for an hour, have a cup of soup, and crash. By then, I would be essentially on their time. I loved my American breakfast, tolerated my Japanese box lunch, and usually took a bunch of Japanese senior managers out for dinner and beer. They often had two-hour commutes, but they did love to party. It's amazing how well we worked through the language barrier in karaoke bars!

I had a real management challenge: Our Japanese division was our most profitable one; we had a 75 percent market share in automotive electrostatic coating; our engineers co-patented new products with our best automotive customers; our division president was ready to retire (not by his assessment, though); no one spoke English; and I was on my own.

I was able to pull off the change at the top; Mickey Ito, who had gone to college in the U.S., had not managed a company before, but he was an effective communicator and a fast study of the changes we wanted to make. On almost every trip, I traveled outside Tokyo to visit our small plants, but I mostly met with customers, which was always a "ceremony," from exchanging business cards to saying good-bye.

Judith was invited to meet the "family" one time when I was discussing licensing arrangements, and we were introduced to Japanese-style bathing where the host "washes" the guest. Business is done during the bathing! We were introduced to sleeping on tatami mats after being entertained at two-hour feasts complete with geisha girls. We had one of our annual Ransburg management meetings in the foothills of magnificent Mt. Fuji, a backdrop I'll never forget!

TRAVELING THE WORLD

In between my regular trips to Japan, I worked in Brazil, Australia, India, China, and Europe. But Brazil frustrated me throughout my career. I just couldn't put the deals together that would have made for a great partnership!

China was an enigma from the beginning! I didn't speak Chinese and had very little experience with the culture. I will never forget being summoned by the minister of trade in Beijing; they were interested in powder coating 50 million bicycles! This was just after the student uprising in 1989 that was centered in Tiananmen Square. The hotels were nearly empty, but the Chinese were very hospitable, and after our very ceremonial business meeting, I was turned loose in their "private" museum and came home with a lovely large ceramic tricolored Chinese horse! It sat proudly in our doorway in Carmel and then on Kiawah Island. Mysteriously, it did not survive our subsequent move to Washington, D.C.

I loved our Swiss operation in St. Gallen. It had beautiful countryside and just the right balance of French and German influence. We were delighted to support the printing of a nearby abbey's book and won a lot of friends that way.

I particularly liked visiting our much larger German operation near Frankfurt; the people were great and I found a charming old hotel outside the city that specialized in white asparagus when it was in season. I ordered it three meals a day! In those days, I regularly did red-eye flights so I could arrive on Monday mornings. However, my flights to Frankfurt always ended up with my arriving on Saturday to coincide with the times when asparagus was at its peak.

MENTOR AND FRIEND

John Nichols proved to be the best mentor I had in my business career. He was bright, demanding, and fun to do business with. My introduction to him came through mutual friends. John's wife, Alexandra, and my friend's wife had worked at Bloomingdale's together and the four of them spent summers in the Hamptons for years. John and Alexandra cared deeply about art and music, were devoted to their two children, and participated actively in Chicago's cultural scene.

MORE ACQUISITIONS

Nichols was inspired by the people, products, and customers at Ransburg. He was intrigued with the company's competitive positions and our ability to deliver customer solutions worldwide. And he urged me to look at acquiring companies that would complement Ransburg.

We first approached Binks Manufacturing, which was headquartered in Franklin Park, Illinois, with an unsolicited offer of $45 a share. When that was rejected by their board, ITW withdrew its offer the day after it expired and on March 7, 1990, announced that it had entered into an agreement with Eagle Industries to acquire Eagle's DeVilbiss division. Terms of the agreement were not disclosed, but each company's annual sales were about $200 million. ITW was accused of having a "hidden agenda in the furtherance of its objectives and nonpublic agenda to acquire another company."

The deal was done with Eagle over one weekend with Eagle contacting ITW. In fact, the possible combination had been approved a year before under the Hart-Scott-Rodino Antitrust Improvement Act when ITW and Eagle were intensively bidding for Ransburg. Headquartered in Toledo, Ohio, DeVilbiss also had operations in Canada, the United Kingdom, West Germany, France, Brazil, Mexico, and Japan. What a change for Nichols, who claimed he never wanted to get involved in public bidding—and with Sam Zell, of all people!

For me, it was time to evaluate management and product strategies and integrate DeVilbiss and Ransburg as best

I could. While I was doing that, we also acquired BGK Finishing Systems, which specialized in infrared curing solutions for a full range of coatings and was located north of Minneapolis. In 1991 I was also appointed executive vice president of Illinois Tool Works in addition to my Ransburg positions.

CONSIDERING OUR OPTIONS

In 1992, as I approached my sixty-third birthday, Judith asked one day, "Have you ever considered where you'd like to live and then find a company *there* you'd like to run?" I had to admit that it was a novel idea!

We considered the options for our next home and what would best suit our cultural sensibilities and our family's needs. We had never lived further west than Indianapolis and were anxious to get back to the East Coast where much of our family still lived. We needed a strong cultural center with convenient travel and wanted to be reasonably close to many of our children.

In the end, we selected, of all places, Washington, D.C. Brian was now enrolled in tenth grade in Mercersburg Academy and Amanda would enter the Field School in D.C. on February 8, 1993; our older children were mostly in the east and we had a vacation home on Kiawah Island, South Carolina. So the nation's capital seemed to work well for our logistics, and we loved the architecture and art of the city.

Besides, I felt that I had done what I could in developing the Ransburg/ITW finishing business. So I met with John

Nichols to advise him that I would step down around the end of January 1993.

While in Indianapolis, I had joined the Indiana National Bank board of directors, which became the National Bank of Detroit during my tenure. I also served on the board of trustees of Butler University for two years while in Indianapolis and started a long association with the National Art Museum of Sport, which had moved to Indianapolis from Connecticut in 1989.

Additionally, I was invited to join the board of directors of Turner Corporation in 1990 and continued to serve on that board through 1999, when the company was acquired by Hochtief, a German construction firm. Judith served on the boards of the Indianapolis Museum of Art and the Indianapolis Symphony Orchestra, where she chaired the orchestra's major fund-raiser in 1991, as well as serving as the liaison for the Ensemble Music Society, bringing world-class musical ensembles to Indianapolis. So Indianapolis had been good to us. We grew, made many new friends, and enjoyed the time we were there.

LIFE WAITS FOR NO ONE

Judith and I will never forget October 2, 1991, the day she was diagnosed with breast cancer. Our lives screeched to a halt temporarily, but thanks to outstanding medical attention, wonderful friends, and Judith's indomitable determination, it all worked out, and she continues to be cancer free to this day!

VENTURES AND ADVENTURES IN D.C.

Judith took on two challenging and fulfilling opportunities in Washington, D.C.: music librarian at the Washington National Cathedral and research assistant at the Smithsonian American Art Museum, later becoming acting curator for the museum's photography collection. That kept her out of trouble! In 1992, thanks in large part to the encouragement of George Steinbrenner, I was elected as a public sector director of the United States Olympic Committee.

At the time, this was an unwieldy organization trying to represent athletes and the national governing bodies of the various sports, and it was largely dependent on television revenues to cover its roughly $400 million quadrennial budget. There were only four public sector directors, and we were supposed to represent the best interests of the public. I had the best job: chairman of the Audit Committee for two terms until 2000, which provided a wonderful behind-the-scenes window on the Olympics.

FOUNDING ADVISORY
CAPITAL PARTNERS

While still trying to identify the "right job" in the Washington area, I became associated with Scott Newquist and Bob Eccles, and helped to found Advisory Capital Partners, an investment advising service. Newquist had been a managing partner at Morgan Stanley and an executive managing director of Kidder Peabody. Eccles had joined the faculty at the

Harvard Business School in 1979 and left in 1993 to found Advisory Capital Partners before returning to his position at Harvard in 2007

For several years, I have enlisted Bob's counsel in my work in sustainable value creation, where he is a leading authority in improving corporate reporting, and has written several books on the subject. As the vice chair of Advisory Capital Partners from 1993 to 1994, I focused on business development, corporate advising, and raising capital for our first fund. But most large investors are reluctant to invest in first-time funds, which made it somewhat difficult to fulfill our stated goal.

Chapter 8

ACADEMIA AND ATHLETICS

High achievement always takes place in the framework
of high expectation.

—CHARLES KETTERING

A SUDDEN CHANGE

Judith and I were attending a Tower Club dinner in New York City in the spring of 1994 when the conversation turned to the subject of the search for a new athletic director at Cornell. From across the table, Harvey Sampson boomed, "Charlie, you should be the next AD!"

Laing Kennedy had resigned his post as Cornell's sixth AD in February and that, along with a continuing string of weak team performances, anchored our table conversation that evening. Sampson, a classmate, a friend, a lineman when Cornell had nationally ranked football teams, a distinguished trustee, and a passionately loyal and generous alumnus, had a way of forcefully making his point.

But I had many reasons why I couldn't consider his suggestion: I was too old (sixty-five), had no athletic administration experience, already had a job, and, most important, had committed to Judith that we would stay in Washington, D.C., where our daughter was a senior in high school and Judith was deeply involved in her work.

But we worked our way through those issues because I was intrigued at the thought of returning to my alma mater and aggressively tackling what might turn out to be the most challenging turnaround yet. It also helped that Brian had just enrolled as a freshman at Cornell.

I was selected after several rounds of interviews, and the announcement was made on October 20, 1994, ahead of the annual trustee and council meetings in Ithaca.

Judith and Amanda would stay in Washington, D.C., until Amanda graduated from the Field School. All of the other children had long since flown the coop.

Happily, Barlow Ware, an iconic fixture in the Cornell Development Office, took me in until we could regroup and prepare to move to Ithaca. I officially started on November 28 but actually got moving right after the press release in October, more excited than I had ever been about a new challenge!

THE NEED FOR A NEW VISION

The Department of Athletics and Physical Education had 120 full-time employees, 34 intercollegiate sports, and a budget of $10 million. But a new vision was essential to improve the attitudes of the student athletes, coaches, and alumni. Cornell had just settled a gender-equity suit, dropped two men's sports, had a record of budget shortfalls, and had too many losing teams as well as some gaps in competitive facilities. I was determined to improve communications and relations between Cornell's seven undergraduate colleges and Big Red sports, and I began by working with the academic deans.

A GOOD FIRST DAY ON THE JOB

On my first whirlwind day, I went to several practices, ending up with the women's fencing team, which had no dedicated facility and had lost their male counterparts through a recently settled Title IX suit.[1]

After practice, we went for pizza, where I got an earful of concerns and suggestions. A woman fencer from Malaysia, Nina Kamaria Farouk, suggested that her mother might be willing to help fund a new fencing salle for both men and women, and I inquired as to how best to communicate with her mother.

Armed with a fax number, I boldly asked for $750,000! The very next morning I received an apologetic response; she could only send $500,000, which was immediately wire transferred! With some additional financial support from other very generous families, we were on our way to building and dedicating a new fencing salle! A great start!

---

1 The government mandate for equal treatment for women in athletics.

SPURRING IMPROVEMENTS TO
THE EQUESTRIAN PROGRAM

Inspired by the challenges of offering equal opportunity for women (half of Cornell's student population), I introduced a varsity equestrian program because we already had a cherished history in men's and women's polo complete with a polo hall and extensive stables. I was surprised to learn how many students bring their horses to Cornell with them. This spurred me to get the funding for upgrading the Oxley Equestrian Center and improve many of our other equestrian services.

CREATIVE WAYS TO FUND ATHLETICS

One of the most popular ways I found to build financial support and allegiance to a sport is through endowing the head coach's position as well as other positions. I also found that this "collegiality" could be reinforced through annual recognition and celebratory dinners.

Still, you don't please everyone. One of my most controversial moves was a restructuring initiative that began in the spring of 1996. The plan called for four men's varsity sports—baseball, tennis, lightweight crew, and lightweight (now called "sprint") football—to go from department-funded to self-funded status.

The reality was that I had to choose between eliminating some sports or making internal changes. I felt my "self-funding" approach was better than cutting athletic opportunities. As it happened, all four of the affected sports have recorded great success, including Ivy League titles, after caring alumni and parents stepped up to support their own or their children's favorite sport.

Better communications with all constituencies was key, so I started publishing *Spirit!*, a slick informative sports magazine designed and run by Barbara Mingle. We didn't have the funds in the beginning to do this, but because it proved essential to "friend-raising" as well as fund-raising, we pressed ahead. That publication continues to provide great coverage of all Cornell sports, their schedules and stars, as well as illustrating a greatly expanded roster of giving categories.

OTHER COST-CUTTING MEASURES

Other cost-cutting changes, mostly mandated by the university, weren't quite so visible, such as eliminating or restructuring department administrative positions. Early on, I insisted on establishing realistic budgets for our programs so that members of the coaching staff would have the resources to offer a first-rate experience for our athletes and the participants in other programs like outdoor education and the Big Red band. This decision still remains fundamental to the success of our teams and programs as loyal and generous friends of the Big Red have lifted their annual operating support from $1.5 million to more than $5 million.

A TURNING POINT

Three and a half years into my "immersion" in Cornell athletics and physical education, I was ready to stand up and be heard! I had undertaken, with the help of the other Ivy ADs, a comparative survey of program costs and university support. It was not a rosy picture! I would have to initiate an unpopular battle.

Although the average Ivy university's support as a percentage of total program costs was 50 percent, Harvard's was 75 percent and Cornell's was 25 percent. It turns out that I had signed on as a fund-raiser, not just an athletic director.

So I prevailed on Harold Tanner, the chairman of the board of trustees, to let me address the central issues standing in the way of achieving real distinction in athletics—real success in varsity sports—that I believed that every Cornellian wanted and deserved.

At the outset of my speech to the trustees, I conceded that our mission at Cornell was, and has always been, academic excellence.

> However, the broad range of physical culture, for which I am accountable, makes a tremendous difference in the overall student experience at Cornell. It also makes a tremendous difference to alumni, potential students, and to nearly all of us who work here. Cornell is a far better place because of the athletic, physical, and outdoor education, and the intramural, fitness, and wellness programs offered across the campus. While only one percent of the university's total annual operating budget is devoted to this broad range of physical culture, the programs and those who administer the programs touch every single student.

I conceded that Cornell's performance in intercollegiate athletics had been "less than impressive" (fifth out of eight in men's and women's Ivy championships). While Cornell had the largest undergraduate Ivy League population, I revealed that we were last in media standings, last in the overall academic "scores" of entering freshmen, and next to last in the academic "scores" of new student athletes. I also pointed out that the spread between the academic "scores" of new student athletes and the rest of the incoming students was the smallest at Cornell and the largest at Princeton—not a coincidence, in my opinion, as this showed that there were special admissions policies at Princeton to attract certain student athletes.

With information from records maintained by the Council of Ivy Group Presidents but (I suspect) not studied by the Cornell trustees, I went on to report that Cornell ranked last in "yield" (the percentage of students who matriculate compared to those offered admission) for both general students and student athletes.

By now, I had their attention. I saw this as a challenge and an opportunity, and told them so as I outlined four essential initiatives concerning admissions, alumni, funding, and new competitive levels.

I told the trustees that I had been consistently urging the administration, and now I was urging them, to stop accepting mediocrity: "Cornell can and must make a commitment to athletic excellence . . . I believe that substantially improved intercollegiate results should be a key university priority."

I also suggested that the dean of admissions or the director of athletics be entrusted with a certain number of admits to be used to attract key male and female athletes—with minimum academic standards established in advance. I told the trustees that this was working at other Ivy schools and that if Cornell was going to be competitive, it must find a workable solution to consistently admit and enroll the best student athletes.

After discussing an issue that didn't have a price tag, I then moved to one that did: adequate funding for our programs in athletics and physical education.

I explained that we had held costs on men's programs to an 11 percent increase over the last three years while having to increase spending on women's programs by 73 percent to remove inequities and comply with Title IX and achieve "substantial proportionality" in intercollegiate participation opportunities.

I also spoke of the changing needs of students and the changing makeup of the university that required additional investments in nonvarsity programs and suggested that these investments be shared by the university, the alumni, and special revenue-producing programs initiated by the department.

Finally, I suggested that it was reasonable to expect more support from alumni *if* we deserved it by pulling ourselves out of the cellar of "perennial losers," and that this would require a university-wide commitment to athletic excellence.

We are at a decisive crossroad. You can sense my frustration. You should be frustrated, too, as should the administration. I am not suggesting that we act out of frustration, but I am suggesting that we act!

As for you trustees, (1) you need to stay informed about the needs and success of physical culture at Cornell, (2) you need to commit to improved admission of student athletes, and (3) you need to support prudent investments in our programs that offer Cornell's students safe, competitive, equitable, and challenging opportunities to express and enrich themselves in a wide range of physical culture. I am committed to carrying out these programs. I am also committed to excellence. To me, that is spelled w-i-n-n-i-n-g.

I sat down not knowing what to expect next, noting that President Hunter Rawlings's face looked awfully red.

THE AFTERMATH

What happened was this: I was greeted with a standing ovation, the chair dispensed with questions, thanked and excused me, and the trustees went into executive session. I was told later that they formed the Trustee Task Force for Athletics, chaired by Bob Kennedy (the former chair and CEO of Union Carbide), to investigate my revelations and allegations, and come back to the board with recommendations.

The Athletic Department, along with the dean of admissions and various directors of college admissions, met with this task force over the next six months and confirmed everything I had said in my presentation.

Their recommendation to the board of trustees was to adopt all three of my recommendations on admits, alumni, and university funding as well as endorse my aspiration for new competitive levels.

I was never invited back to speak to the board, but then I never had to again. Based on what I have heard from Cornell trustees over the years, substantially improved intercollegiate results, admits, and university funding are still considered priorities.

During my five years as athletic director, I was particularly proud of the number of athletic facilities we constructed or upgraded, including the Friedman Strength and Conditioning Center, the Kane Sports Complex, new outdoor tennis courts at the Reis Tennis Center, improvements at the Oxley Equestrian Center, the Niemand-Robison Softball Field, the Stifle Fencing Salle, new international-standard squash courts, and a new irrigation system and golf center for the Robert Trent Jones Golf Course.

REWARDING RELATIONSHIPS

A profoundly rewarding dimension of my duties as athletic director was interacting with the donors, their heirs, and other critical actors who bring sports to life in a big school.

Sanford Reis and his son, Curtis, had attended the 1952 Olympics, sailing to Helsinki on the MS *Batory* with my family and throwing a celebratory party on board after I won, and who later helped Cornell improve its tennis facilities.

Bob Kane (Cornell's AD from 1941 to 1971) was my hero: a good quarter-miler, an athletic director, the track team manager in Helsinki, a president of USOC, and a true friend whose name appears on the sports complex that includes the William E. Simon Track (Simon followed Kane as president of the USOC), the Carl A. Kroch Throwing Fields, the Charles F. Berman Field (named for one of my fraternity brothers), and a 1,000-seat stadium.

Judith and I commissioned a piece of sculpture to represent the activities of the Kane Sports Complex that now stands at the front gate of the center. We chose sculptor Joel Perlman, who received his BFA from Cornell in 1965. His work in metal sculpture had historically been composed of straight lines and angles without any circles. Judith argued for including circles that would echo the balls, hockey pucks, and hoops that represented some of Cornell's sports. The result was that much of Perlman's recent work now includes circles.

One of the most critical things I learned as athletic director is the importance of coaches. They recruit the best athletes who can also cope with the academic challenges at Cornell. They are the ones who can inspire performances beyond expectations. They are the ones who build the necessary staff, manage budgets, and encourage alumni support.

In short, they are Cornell ambassadors for their sport.

When I arrived in Ithaca, we didn't have the best coaches; some hadn't had a winning season in years. When I met with those coaches, I asked if their athletes were having good experiences. The answer was consistently no, which opened a dialogue about why this was.

The coaches took most of the blame and asked for help in improving or, more often, for my help in finding them something they could be more successful at. This resulted in twenty-one varsity head coaches being hired in my first four years, including five who were promoted from within the ranks.

But my favorite memory is my interaction with the student athletes. I found it inordinately energizing to work with groups like the Student-Athlete Advisory Council, which I had to revitalize, and the Red Key Society.

A PROUD LEGACY

I have always had an open-door policy, which student athletes took advantage of often in the wee hours. With the crazy hours students so often keep, they did their strength training and practicing around the clock; and more often than not, they found me in my office in Teagle Hall ready to listen. And they were seldom bashful in sharing their recommendations!

One day during ordinary working hours, a coach came in to share his concern for the academic standing of one of his athletes and brought with him the complete GPA listing of all our varsity athletes. As I scanned this list of more than 1,100 athletes, I saw a 4.0 and then another and another. I soon realized that Cornell had more than forty varsity athletes who were carrying a 4.0 or higher grade point average. Nothing in my own experience had prepared me to expect this level of proficiency.

This was the birth of Cornell's 400 Club!

I immediately called President Rawlings to request that he reserve one morning each semester to have breakfast with the new club and the academic provost.

I was fascinated by the fact that every student athlete told essentially the same story. They loved their exercise, their studies, and Cornell, often in that order. Even though their physical and competitive activities were essential to them, they had also come to Cornell to pursue their studies. Their challenge was in balancing the two.

This breakfast still occurs; and I suspect the president and provost have been the real beneficiaries. President David Skorton (Cornell's twelfth president and now the Secretary of the Smithsonian Institution) once devoted his editorial in *Cornell* magazine to the 400 Club!

FAMILY LIFE

Another special memory of Cornell and Ithaca is the house where my family and I lived.

Early in the summer of 1995, following Amanda's graduation, we took up residence at 630 Highland Road. The house was a large Tudor-style that had been built by the same architect who designed the president's house on Cayuga Heights Road.

It had been purchased by the house's one-time paperboy who was now a successful investment banker living in Hong Kong. Because he was a Cornellian and loved Cornell athletics, Warren Alderidge was very pleased to rent us his home with any furniture we wanted (including his collection of Oriental rugs!) for as long as we needed it. A bonus was the fact that his brother, Paul, was the designated caretaker and would do all the snowplowing, grass mowing, and window washing, which was included in our very reasonable rent.

We have been very fortunate to live in some terrific homes over the years while we chased turnarounds, but 630

Highland Road may well be my favorite. It had every possible requirement for a large active family and an athletic director who loved to entertain large numbers of Cornell alumni, athletic teams, and his family.

New and old friends greatly enhanced our stay in Ithaca. Our friendship with Charles and Margo Treman, our neighbors on Highland Road, remains unforgettable; Charlie was class of 1930, the captain of his track team, a trustee, and a distinguished head judge (always dressed in tails and top hat) at indoor track meets.

When Brian decided to go for his electrical engineering master's degree, he lived in the bedroom over the garage, and we saw him frequently for meals and always on laundry day.

PRAISE, REFLECTIONS, AND WINDING DOWN

But all good things come to an end, and I had been clear from the beginning that I would stay only for five years.

On January 7, 1999, the *Ithaca Journal* announced, "Energetic Moore to Retire: Oversaw great growth; Cornell aiming to have a successor hired by July." Susan Murphy, the vice president for student and academic services I reported to, was quoted in the article.

> Moore has an amazing energy level. His days are long. They start early and go late . . . Moore was hired to oversee a time of great change, especially from a financial standpoint. The athletic department

I was always a cheerleader when I was "CEO of Athletics" at Cornell from 1994 to 1999.

budget hadn't been balanced in a decade prior to his arrival. [I know of] no person who has a greater passion or more energy than he does. He's been a very enthusiastic ambassador for Cornell athletics!

President Rawlings was also quoted.

Charlie Moore has done a superb job. He has appointed outstanding coaches, built state-of-the-art new facilities, led major initiatives in our women's programs and developed considerable alumni support. We have an excellent and balanced set of programs as a result of his dedicated efforts, for which all Cornellians are grateful.

My response?

> I couldn't be more positive about the direction in which we're headed. This has been absolutely the greatest experience of my life. I wouldn't have given it up for anything. While I have worked hard, I've gotten out far more than I've put in.

And all of that was true; I did have the time of my life. What's not to like about having more than 1,100 student athletes as your new best friends and helping to develop a plan that goes well beyond a university's athletic win-loss records and encompasses student evaluations of the physical education program, student participation in intramural sports, and the academic performance of student athletes?

SAYING GOOD-BYE AND HELLO

Now, at the age of seventy, I had to finish out my term at Cornell, help in the national search for my successor, and start thinking about my next job! Fortunately, I had attracted a terrific administrative staff that included two outstanding associate athletic directors.

One of them, Andy Noel, a former wrestling coach at Cornell, eventually got my position and is still doing a great job there; my other associate, Dianne Murphy, took the top athletic post at Denver and then moved on to be athletic director of Columbia University. What satisfaction: to be involved in preparing 25 percent of the Ivy League ADs!

When Heidrick & Struggles called to ask what I knew about corporate philanthropy, I had to admit that I knew very little but that I had a lot of experience in fund-raising. After more discussions and interviews, I was offered the job of leading a start-up nonprofit headquartered in New York.

That was a problem; we loved Washington. Judith had been commuting back and forth between Ithaca and the nation's capital for four years holding down positions in both the Washington National Cathedral and Smithsonian American Art Museum, and I had committed to return to Washington.

So we compromised; we moved back to Washington to another rented house and I started commuting to New York City.

We would miss Ithaca and all that my five years of being back at Cornell had entailed. My Cornell experience spanned more than fifty-two years plus these last years of being a proud alumnus!

Chapter 9

BRINGING THE ARTS INTO BUSINESS

Art is like a border of flowers along the course of civilization.

—LINCOLN STEFFENS

TWO-WAY BENEFITS

Businesses spend billions of dollars annually playing a key role in ensuring the health and vitality of the nation's arts sector. This support for the arts is most successful when it is driven less by charitable intent and more by a focus on how the arts impact the communities where the businesses' employees live and work.

My observation is that art is a powerful agent for change and that there is a lot that firms can learn from the power of the image, including how to drive sustainability. That is why David Rockefeller, back in 1967, founded the Business Committee for the Arts, which is still going strong. It's no surprise that Mr. Rockefeller convened his first annual meeting at the Metropolitan Museum of Art in New York City.

While my main driving force in the arts has been my wife, I have also been extremely fortunate to be associated with corporate leaders who helped me support a range of arts in the communities where we had businesses, which translated into enormous success and personal joy.

I never visit corporate headquarters without exploring their art collections and even the art books on their shelves and coffee tables. I look for sculpture when touring their office campuses. When possible, I search out their art consultants, which invariably makes a good impression, and I have discovered that American corporations own and display some of the world's finest art.

BUDGETING FOR GIVING TO THE ARTS

The BCA National Survey of Business Support for the Arts, which is produced by Americans for the Arts, indicates that 47 percent of total business contributions come from small businesses with philanthropy budgets under $1 million. Contributions from midsize businesses represent another 35 percent of the total.

Large companies that are featured in most business pages, with philanthropy budgets of more than $50 million, represent only 18 percent of total arts contributions. Given the high percentage of smaller businesses making arts contributions, this indicates that the number of businesses participating is quite high and very much based in localities all across the country rather than coming from a few big corporations.

This same BCA survey shows that the bulk of donations from businesses today comes from advertising or marketing budgets while a smaller amount comes from philanthropy budgets. These percentages have flipped over the last decade. The data indicate that contributing to the arts is seen not only as a good thing to do for the community as a whole but also as a valuable business strategy for the company.

WHY BUSINESS LEADERS GIVE (AND DON'T GIVE)

Business leaders participating in this survey were asked to identify their principal reasons for giving. The most common were to improve the quality of life in a community, create a more vibrant society, and improve academic performance. Survey participants also argued that arts organizations offered education initiatives that benefit the community. It's clear that the concept of community captures the essence of why businesses enthusiastically support the arts.

But it is interesting to note that 72 percent of the businesses surveyed that currently give to the arts said that the number one reason they might increase contribution levels was if they felt profitability could be improved because of that additional investment. And the number one reason (66 percent) that businesses mentioned for not giving to the arts is that they were never asked to.

When I was part of the Committee Encouraging Corporate Philanthropy, we developed a corporate giving standard, and our annual survey showed that those companies participating consistently apportioned 5 percent of their annual giving to culture and the arts. This is somewhat misleading because our survey was heavily weighted toward Fortune 500 companies.

INTERPACE CORPORATE GIVING

Bill Hartman cared deeply about art, and Interpace already had an extensive collection in place when he joined the company in 1974. In 1978 Interpace retained Phillips B. van Dusen of Contributions Management in order to:

1. Measurably improve its reputation as a smart, creative, high-quality, and prudent company in the eyes of the press and Wall Street
2. Enhance the company's recognition among employees, local leaders, and potential acquisitions as a thoughtful, community-minded corporation
3. Become known as *the* corporation devoted to the support of a hitherto ignored art form—sculpture, and American sculpture in particular
4. Gain recognition (and set an example for others) as a company committed to private support of the arts

The premise for this commitment was based on the fact that every company is different, that management should use all publicly expended funds (including contributions) to gain recognition, and that these contributions should be planned, scrutinized, and be every bit as creative in fulfilling corporate objectives as any other investment of shareholder assets. It was also felt that a company should support the arts, or any other nonprofit area, only if that support helped achieve corporate goals and allowed the company to take all reasonable credit for its investments.

In short, I learned that every company can benefit from well-managed contributions, a lesson that I would carry with me through the rest of my operating responsibilities, including my years at CECP. Coincidentally, most of my building-products portfolio at Interpace contained objects that resembled contemporary sculpture!

INTERPACE AND MOMA

With Hartman's enthusiastic endorsement and van Dusen's brilliant sleuth work, Interpace first connected with the Museum of Modern Art in New York, whose board represents one of the bastions of American financial leadership. The timing was perfect. To reinforce our strategy built around sculpture, we underwrote the planting, care, and feeding of seasonal flowers in MoMA's sculpture garden, which was many New Yorkers' favorite quiet spot in the city.

In addition, we provided funding for green plants in the lobby. This came with permanent signage crediting the flora to Interpace and a monthly credit in the members' newsletter. And we were offered the opportunity to underwrite MoMA's huge retrospective of their own contemporary sculpture that would take place in the middle of MoMA's eighteen-month-long fiftieth-anniversary celebration. Great visibility for Interpace!

We also hosted a series of five receptions in the sculpture garden for selected guests and strategic customers. The press coverage Interpace received was gratifying and surprised everyone.

These were modest gestures compared to what came next. But they opened doors and our company's mind to the possibilities.

Without identifying the client or any specific interest in sculpture, van Dusen approached Philippe de Montebello, the director of the Metropolitan Museum of Art. And his timing could not have been more perfect!

A call had just come from Paris asking for help in mounting an exhibition of fragments from eleventh-century sculptures taken from the façade of Notre Dame during the French Revolution. Mistaking the statues of biblical kings for those of the kings of France, vandals beheaded the sculptures and tossed them into a pile of debris in front of the famous church. These fragments were discovered in 1977 buried under the courtyard of a Paris bank. This discovery was a historic event, and the small but elegant exhibition was a treasure!

The Met and the Cleveland Museum of Art were offered an exhibition of thirteen of these pieces that would then be permanently installed at the Cluny museum in Paris. The timing for Interpace was ideal as our projects at MoMA were finishing. And *Sculpture from Notre Dame, Paris: A Dramatic Recovery* was to be a "banner" show at the Met. Hartman responded with the needed funding, and the show opened to rave reviews.

The *Wall Street Journal* applauded Interpace for "its methods and motives." Philippe de Montebello spoke at our celebratory dinner, and his introduction to the catalog credited the "generous funding from Interpace Corporation" that made the exhibition possible.

EXTENDING INTERPACE'S REACH

In five short months, Interpace had put its imprimatur on the world of sculpture. But there was more to come as a result of Interpace's recently developed reach and reputation: underwriting scholarships to a sculpture conference in Washington, D.C., a PBS film on the American sculptor Isamu Noguchi, and outdoor environmental exhibitions at Interpace's hometown museum in Morristown, New Jersey.

By this time, Interpace firmly believed that private support of the arts could benefit artists, museums, *and* corporate sponsors (infinitely more so when combined with government support); and they were looking for ways to take sculpture exhibitions to cities that had company plants. The goals were to establish the divisions and Interpace in the community and impress employees with the value of the company's support of sculpture.

THE AMERICAN EIGHT

Eventually, van Dusen and CMI focused on ConStruct, an association of young American sculptors led by Mark di Suvero that included Charles Ginnever, John Raymond Henry,

Linda Howard, Lyman Kipp, Frank McGuire, Jerry Peart, and Kenneth Snelson. They called their traveling exhibition of participatory contemporary sculpture *American Eight*, and their work was big and required semis and large lifting equipment to move it around.

Interpace mounted it in five cities that had company facilities. The plants were all under my leadership and all of them produced building products, most of which have a sculptural look and feel.

Every *American Eight* show was a major community event. The cost averaged $22,300 per exhibition, including transportation, insurance, installation and removal, and artists' seminars. We estimated that our investment came to $23.80 per thousand visitors. That's not much for the visibility and publicity the exhibitions provided. You can't please everyone, however, as one visitor to the Memorial Art Gallery in Rochester complained that he thought the museum had gone into the "scrap-yard business."

THE VALUE OF DESIGN

In the process of acquiring Torin Corporation, I visited their facilities in Torrington, Connecticut, a number of times. You knew immediately that something unique was happening there. I soon discovered that all the company's buildings were designed by the same person, the noted Hungarian architect Marcel Breuer. This special client-architect relationship had started in 1952, the year before construction began on Breuer's Paris headquarters for UNESCO.

Breuer, who was associated with Bauhaus, Walter Gropius, and modernism, is known in New York City as the designer of the former Whitney Museum of American Art, now called the Met Breuer after it was leased in 2016 by the Metropolitan Museum of Art.

Incidentally, Breuer's first building for Torin was a one-story 12,000-square-foot plant for its Canadian operation. In 1954 he designed a 50,000-square-foot building in Van Nuys, California. By then, Andrew Gagarin was Torin's president, and he and Breuer were intrigued by the possibility of utilizing a system of long-span hyperbolic paraboloids to minimize the number of columns on a factory floor. Similar constructions using preformed concrete panels followed in Indiana, Belgium, and the United Kingdom.

In Torrington, the Naugatuck River winds through the city and is edged by the usual turn-of-the-century construction. Torin housed its machine division in a multistory building of red brick from that period that doglegged to fit the river. In 1962 the decision was made to house this function on a single floor and combine the factory with office space and laboratories.

I was particularly impressed with their technical center that was built in 1971. This latest construction was my favorite because of its space and scale and its multiuse and visual harmony. It illustrates Breuer's classic sense of form and Torin's commitment over twenty years to quality and adding something beautiful to the world.

SUPPORTING THE ARTS
THROUGH COLLECTING

But Torin's commitment to the arts didn't stop at architecture. Gagarin and Rufus Stillman, the Torin chairman at the time of our acquisition, had a great eye and love for art, and also relied on the advice of Ivan Chermayeff, the prolific designer, illustrator, and artist. Ivan was a founding partner of Chermayeff & Geismar & Haviv, a leading graphic design firm in the fields of corporate identity, brand development, and logo design. Ivan designed the iconic logos for the Smithsonian Institution, MoMA, Pan Am, Mobil, and, of course, Torin. (Ivan would also design our first Clevepak annual report.)

Artists in Torin's extraordinary collection included Alexander Calder, Josef Albers, Erastus Dow Palmer (a marble sculpture that is now in the Met's collection), Pablo Picasso, and Roy Lichtenstein.

When Clevepak moved to new expanded headquarters, 161 pieces of the Torin art collection, appraised at over $300,000, were relocated throughout hallways and private offices. Ivan Chermayeff graciously agreed to oversee the mounting of this artwork. The sleek new lobby reception area afforded visitors the opportunity to browse through Clevepak brochures and study the unique sculpture collection.

We chose to emphasize sculpture in our lobby for two reasons: it is a natural analogue to many of our manufactured products, and there is an increasing need for corporate support for American sculpture.

In November 1984, Manhattanville College conducted an art history seminar in the Clevepak offices to review issues concerning corporate support for the arts and study the sculpture collection with a particular focus on the problems of installation in public places.

We never gave serious consideration to liquidating the Torin art collection after the acquisition. Clevepak saw art as a true expression of creativity, believing that including art in our working environment served as a steady reminder that creativity is critical to each of our jobs.

ACQUISITION MEANS REEXAMINING VALUES

With Clevepak's acquisition of Interpace in August 1983, we had to decide whether or not to continue with Contributions Management and Interpace's various commitments to museums. But it was not a difficult decision. As we grew more knowledgeable and focused more on American sculpture, CMI identified an area that had been mostly ignored by the art world: early American sculpture.

Hartman encouraged CMI to find ways to recognize the richness of early American sculpture and further Interpace's growing reputation as an educated corporate supporter of the arts.

A partnership with the outstanding Department of American Art at the University of Delaware was developed in early 1982 to publish the definitive scholarly study of the entire field and mount an exhibition based on that work.

CLEVEPAK AND AMERICAN SCULPTURE AT THE METROPOLITAN MUSEUM OF ART

The choir rail and pulpit that once graced All Angels' Church on West Eightieth Street in New York City was carved by Karl Bitter and is considered a leading example of nineteenth-century architecture and religious sculpture in the United States. It had languished in the recesses of the Met until Interpace and the museum found mutual interest and value in it.

The pulpit is now mounted in the northwest corner of Engelhard Court in the American wing of the Met. It commands your attention from the moment you enter, and it always will, for as the sign below the pulpit explains, this is a permanent installation made possible by a grant from Interpace Corporation.

From October 1983 to January 1984, the American wing mounted, with Clevepak as the sponsor, the first one-man show since 1856 of the works of Erastus Dow Palmer. Curated by Donna Hassler, this exhibition featured twenty-five of the finest examples of the work of this American neoclassic sculptor.

Our second Clevepak exhibition at the Met, curated by Lewis Sharp, ran from March 24 to May 19, 1985, and featured the sculpture of John Quincy Adams Ward.

A PRIVATE SHOWING

Soon after the exhibition opened, we hosted a private showing and black-tie dinner for fifty in honor of Prescott and

Beth Bush. Prescott, a Greenwich neighbor, was the older brother of George H. W. Bush, who had recently been inaugurated as vice president.

All attendees agreed that it was "without question one of the most perfect evenings we have had in New York City." Many of the guests were CEOs who recognized Clevepak's exemplary support of American sculpture and wondered why more companies didn't understand the merit of such support. It was such a successful party that we had to pay overtime for the eleven regular museum guards and four special policemen!

OUR GREATEST AND LAST
EXHIBIT AT THE MET

It is almost universally agreed that no American sculptor of the late nineteenth or early twentieth century compares to Augustus Saint-Gaudens, the subject of our concluding trifecta of exhibitions at the Met. It was surprising to learn, therefore, that in 1985 there had been no major exhibition of his work in more than seventy-five years.

Our final exhibition at the Met included sixty of the sculptor's finest works, including delicately carved cameos and preliminary studies for *The Puritan*, *Standing Lincoln*, the *Adams Memorial* (my absolute favorite), and the golden statue of Diana that stood atop Stanford White's Madison Square Garden. Of special interest were the loans of the statue of Admiral David Farragut from Madison Square Park (loaned by the New York City Department of Parks & Recreation)

Kathryn Greenthal, guest curator at the Met, and Judith in front of a Saint-Gaudens relief in 1985.

and a nine-foot-long relief from the Robert Louis Stevenson memorial in St. Giles' Cathedral in Edinburgh.

This exhibition was curated by Kathryn Greenthal, who wrote the definitive book on Saint-Gaudens that accompanied the exhibition. In 1900 Saint-Gaudens found out he had cancer. He gave up his home and studio in New York and moved permanently to his summer house in Cornish, New Hampshire, that overlooked Mount Ascutney, an oasis Judith and I have visited a number of times.

Saint-Gaudens has always been my favorite because of his superb public works and masterly reliefs. He moved American sculpture into a splendid new period of achievement, and Clevepak was fortunate to fund the retrospective showing of his masterpieces.

RECOGNITIONS FOR CONTRIBUTIONS TO THE ARTS

Although Clevepak was acquired in April 1986, our contract with the Met was honored and the show went on! Glowing articles appeared in *Architectural Digest, House & Garden, Antiques* magazine, and *Sculpture Review*, along with the *New York Times* and *Washington Post*. A tribute to Clevepak, along with other "enlightened" corporations, is inscribed prominently on one of the columns on the first floor of the Met, which I always admire on my frequent trips there. Equally pleasing is the Herbert Adams Memorial Medal presented to Clevepak by the National Sculpture Society in 1984 for service to American sculpture.

ART IN BUSINESS IS GOOD BUSINESS

So how do I really feel about corporate support of the arts?

I see it as a situation where everybody wins. CEOs are

not necessarily arts scholars; they are businessmen with marketing skills, a modicum of good taste (I hope!), and an appreciation of the arts. And they appreciate money well spent for a good cause that benefits the corporate donor as well.

Each exhibition I've described had a purpose and provided fine opportunities for entertainment and education. But the support we provided to artists and museums benefited our business as well by providing good public exposure and recognition.

If a company plans its funding projects well, and then monitors and reappraises them and maintains its commitment, one plus one will equal five. The tangible results are impressive. And the intangible results in developing managers and in employee, community, and government relations go on and on.

On a personal note, I was inspired and learned so much from Torin's commitment to architecture and art, as well as Interpace's support of museums and sculptors. Thanks to Judith, I have been grounded in the appreciation of art as we traveled the world exploring museums, cathedrals, and private collections. At one point, we found ourselves on a mission: exploring the subject of musical instruments as portrayed on Roman sarcophagi for Judith's master's thesis at Manhattanville College. Now that's dedication!

You won't be surprised to learn that my favorite art form is sculpture, followed by photography and painting. As I rank my interest in the performing arts, dance is first (both classical and modern), followed by chamber music, theater, and the symphony. Opera trails these, I'm afraid, as it's too complicated and long for this engineer.

The bottom line is that art is a powerful agent for change and innovation! Business can help foster and support the arts—for everyone's benefit.

Art in business is good business!

Chapter 10

THE POWER OF THE NETWORK

The currency of real networking is not greed but generosity.

—KEITH FERRAZZI

Unless you love everybody, you can't sell anybody.

—DICKY FOX, IN *JERRY MAGUIRE*

I approach networking like I do everything else in my life—with aplomb, enthusiasm, and, of course, purpose. The ability to network effectively has become one of my most distinguishing and valued traits. For me, networking has become a non-negotiable necessity.

It wasn't always so. Although one could say the ability to schmooze well is a characteristic exclusive to natural-born extroverts, purpose-driven networking is a learnable behavior. In the beginning, many of my connections came because I was simply at the right place at the right time. Many of the connections I made were through pure luck.

But I learned how to put myself right in the thick of things. I also learned how to strike when the networking iron was hot and how to maintain relationships *that never should have lasted longer than a moment or two.*

The ways in which building and maintaining a vast network have benefited me are many. They range from the immediate and obvious (generating referrals and increasing business opportunities) to the more subtle (collecting advice at just the right time, increasing my confidence, and gaining the satisfaction that comes from helping others).

Jim Fuchs, my roommate at the Olympics, was the consummate networker. He had a list of more than 200 people whom he called each year on their birthdays, and this was only the beginning of his social prowess. From Jim, I learned how indispensable networking can be for business and social relationships. I studied the ways Jim worked room after room, amassing friends, fans, and potential business allies.

From the age of twenty-five on, I was hooked on networking, and I chose to invest a great deal of time and energy into cultivating an array of relationships that have fed my purpose and vision over the years.

Effective, purposeful networking comes with maturity, confidence, and practice. You need to be curious, love connecting facts, have empathy, and be able to use visualization to enhance your ability to recall important memories. This way, networking isn't simply a social act, but a deeply intellectual and emotional practice. The rewards extend far beyond the personal, however, as each new friend brings joy, meaning, and a sense of connection with the world.

As I took on greater professional responsibility and leadership roles, my network has reoriented externally toward the future. I believe this is an essential part of leadership.

One might say I'm a social opportunist, but that isn't exactly the case. Sometimes my connections have come because I was at the right place at the right time. Such as when I met Prince Philip by chance while dining in the Olympic mess hall.

Other times, they have come because of a particular success I've had, such as being invited to the White House because of my dedication to the Olympics.

Yet, at other times, connections have come from steadfastness and much engineering on my part, such as when I reached out again and again to visit the beautiful Olympic Museum in Lausanne and was hosted by Juan Antonio Samaranch, the former head of the International Olympic Committee.

I dedicate my full attention and respect to the important connections in my life no matter how they came to be, and I work hard to maintain them. It is for this reason that many of my brief encounters have turned into lifelong relationships fueled by shared vision and purpose. Others have become the stuff of legend, stories told around the fireplace and cherished forever.

To be a true agent of change, you have to know how to work a room. I challenge you to cultivate more of what you value not just in your actions and decisions but in your relationships as well. Regardless of the intention (exchanging information or connecting for business or social reasons), networking is one of the most important and most purposeful investments of your time you can make.

When you make a connection that complements what is important to you, take notice. Cultivate it. Don't let it go.

Collected here are a few choice examples of connections and experiences that are particularly representative of what I most value in my life: dedication to athletics, philanthropy, and a general love of my fellow man.

TREASURED PEOPLE

George Steinbrenner

Much has been written, and much more will be, about George M. Steinbrenner III. Born July 4, 1930 (my junior by eleven months), in Rocky River, Ohio, he was educated at Culver Military Academy and Williams College and then glorified and vilified as the principal owner of the New York Yankees.

"The Boss" had many passions, friends, and detractors. He was belligerent and seldom subtle, but he was consistently loyal and generous. Much of his life was chronicled by Bill Madden in his book *Steinbrenner: The Last Lion of Baseball*. However, this is the Steinbrenner I knew.

Our fathers were two of the best collegiate high and low hurdlers from 1924 to 1926. Both George and I treasure our copies of the IC4A reports that contain their records for those years.

George always claimed that he was part of a 4x120-yard

high hurdle shuttle relay team that lost to the Cornell team I ran the third leg for at the Penn Relays in 1951. Many years later, George would tease me about knowing me only from the back of my track shorts! I could never confirm that George competed in this event, but it makes a good story anyhow. And George remained a regular spectator at the Penn Relays.

George's role in the United States Olympic Committee is legendary. His Olympic Overview Commission probably saved that organization after two years of reviewing its governance and support for athletes. And George was responsible for my joining the USOC board of directors in 1992.

Nine years later, I became chair of the USOC's bid city task force and George was a steady confidant; his advice was always pertinent as well as confidential.

George was a regular spectator at most Olympic Games, and he demonstrated his love for the athletes by treating them almost like his own children. He also participated in Xerox's celebration of the 100 Golden Olympians, a special part of the 1996 Games in Atlanta that I was honored to be included in.

The Steinbrenner I knew had nothing to do with his original 1973 purchase of the New York Yankees from CBS for less than $10 million (that was a deal!), his 1990 suspension by baseball commissioner Fay Vincent, his love/hate relationship with Billy Martin, or even his seven World Series championships.

Instead, I got to watch baseball games with George, usually in his private box, which was filled with the most wonderful New York Yankees memorabilia and old friends, particularly Yogi Berra. More often than not, George chose to watch the game alone in an adjoining private cubicle. After all, he needed to concentrate on winning. That was everything for him!

My favorite baseball visit with George was at Legends Field in Tampa (now Steinbrenner Field). It was just the two of us, and I went away loaded with Yankee "stuff" and the knowledge of what makes George tick. This insight was reinforced by several luncheons we had in Manhattan with Jim Fuchs. It was always fun when George was the host; everything in the restaurant would come to a complete halt!

The last time I saw George, he invited Judith and me and my fellow Olympians Jim Fuchs, Harrison Dillard, and Lindy Remigino to a game to celebrate my seventy-sixth birthday in 2005. George's health and memory were failing, but he perked up immediately when he started to talk about the Olympics.

In 1982 Steinbrenner attended the funeral of a New York fireman killed in the line of duty. The officer had four boys, and George was struck by the fact that their hopes of getting an education had been made much more difficult since their father had died. How would these young men get college educations?

In typical Steinbrenner fashion, George started the Silver Shield Foundation, which supports the education of the children of firefighters and police officers killed in the line of duty and was led by my dear friend Jim Fuchs until he died in 2010. George contributed the proceeds from a Yankee game to enhance the donations of Silver Shield members, whose number has grown significantly in the past few years. George's generosity knew no bounds, and he often helped children without taking any credit.

The best speech I ever heard George give was at Genesee Community College. I had persuaded him to come to Batavia, New York, to speak to the local chapter of the Eagle Scouts. He arrived in his private plane in the middle of a typical Buffalo snowstorm.

He dutifully put up with the usual press interviews and "rubber chicken" dinner (all the while glaring at me), but when it came time to speak, his demeanor changed as he spoke of his passion for baseball and then turned his attention to the Scouts and their parents. George had been an Eagle Scout in his youth. Speaking without a single note, he was spellbinding.

As a testimony to my friendship with George—or to his forgiveness—he agreed to another speaking engagement twenty years later. In 1995 Steinbrenner agreed to speak at the first Cornell-Penn Trustees' Cup dinner in New York.

As a kid living in the Philadelphia area, I had attended many Cornell-Penn football games on Thanksgiving Day; it was a big deal. And when I was Cornell's athletic director, I was determined to create something that would rival the annual Harvard-Yale football classic.

So Penn's athletic director, Steve Bilsky, and I created the Trustees' Cup and a black-tie dinner to kick off our respective football seasons. The presidents of Cornell and Penn both agreed to attend, along with the football teams, and our dream was launched. By now, Fay Vincent had reinstated George, and he was back "running" the Yankees.

Cornell's own Dick Schaap had just written a scathing piece on George in his latest book, so that ruled him out as a possible emcee. My friend Harvey Sampson, a Big Red footballer from the class of 1951, served ably in that position.

George was on his best behavior, and he shared his experiences as a Big Ten football coach and waxed eloquently about the values of an Ivy League education and its enviable student-athlete experience.

He then pointed his finger at the university presidents, and said, "Now don't you two foul it up!"

That's the Steinbrenner I knew and will always remember.

Jim Fuchs

James Emanuel Fuchs (pronounced *Fewsh*) was my roommate twice and remained a lifelong friend. He enrolled in Yale University in 1944 and was a starting fullback on their football team. Although he weighed 215 pounds, he could run the 100-yard dash in less than 10 seconds.

Sometimes called the "magnificent wreck," Jim was an extraordinary example of how much an individual could do despite injury, illness, and bad luck, and his stories fascinated me. He won a bronze medal in the 1948 London Olympics while having strep throat and a temperature pushing 105 degrees, and he won his second bronze medal in 1952 despite a severely injured hand.

Because of injuries to his legs, his coaches convinced him to concentrate on the shot put and discus. He developed a new

Jim Fuchs (center), George Steinbrenner (right), and I at a USOC board meeting in 1996.

technique in the shot put to compensate for his injuries that he called "the sideways glide." This innovation enabled him to dominate the sport in 1948 and 1949. He won 88 consecutive events, including the IC4A, NCAA, and AAU titles in 1949 and 1950, and he broke his own world records four times.

The May 15, 1950, issue of *Life* magazine had some fun with him when they featured him both competing and seemingly sleeping, and added: "For a man who throws the heavy shot as easily as most men throw a small grapefruit, 6-foot 1¾-inch, 215-pound Jim Fuchs is remarkably susceptible to bodily ailments of all kinds. In four seasons of track and football he has been beset with head colds, a dislocated shoulder, torn stomach muscles, a trick knee and foot blisters." They also rightly observed that the "shot-put champion rarely worries about himself, is relaxed in competition."

I first met Jim when Cornell competed against Yale in an indoor dual meet in Ithaca, where he beat our best sprinter in the 60-yard dash and broke the wall down in the shot put because the officials wouldn't listen to his arguments that there wasn't enough room.

Jim never let me forget the fact that Yale won that meet and went on to win the Ivy League indoor championships that year. In 1952 we both won our events in the indoor AAU championships and were invited to go to Trinidad as ambassadors, coaches, and demonstration competitors for several days. That was the first time I roomed with Jim.

When we both made the 1952 Olympic team, Jim asked if I would like to room with him. That was fine with me as I knew he would be out and about and that I would have our room mostly to myself, which proved to be the case.

Jim spent twenty years as a communications executive, first at NBC, then at Curtis Publishing, and finally as president of Mutual Sports. From 1976 to 1994, Jim was chairman and CEO of Fuchs, Cuthrell & Company, a successful outplacement firm that would play an important role in my life. I not only used their services when I left Interpace in 1981, but Jim insisted that Judith and I relocate to Greenwich instead of Westchester County. That's carrying "outplacement" to an extreme! He was right, of course!

Led by Jim's daughter, the Silver Shield Foundation has been expanded to cover children in New York, New Jersey, and Connecticut and is supported by a number of leading businesspeople, all friends of the "magnificent wreck."

Jim married Anne Sutherland in 1982. Anne had held senior positions at the Hearst Corporation, Condé Nast, and Hachette. She launched *O, The Oprah Magazine* and *Elle* magazine. She once famously said, "If I could invent my day and create whatever I wanted to do—I'm doing it. Jim likes to go out eight nights a week; I like to go out six nights a week; so we've settled on seven."

Anne says that Jim "celebrated sports wherever he went . . . that he would try as hard as possible but if not the winner, he would applaud as the champion ran by. He knew the rules of sports and loved every minute competing, whether in a casual golf game or a significant tournament."

Jim and I competed against each other for years, even in seeing how many coconuts we could grab in the surf of Trinidad as part of our two-man AAU track-ambassador tour. And we played in a number of golf tournaments, where we were always hailed as the "old Olympic roommates."

Sadly, Jim died on October 8, 2010, at the age of eighty-two. But his stories live on, including the one about the time he was kicked out of Central Park in 1952 for making holes in the grass while practicing for the Olympics.

One of his friends defined this great humanitarian as a "man among men." I thought he was pretty terrific, too.

Paul Newman

Paul Leonard Newman, born in Shaker Heights, Ohio, on January 26, 1925, was an actor, a film director, an entrepreneur, a race car driver, an environmentalist, and a philanthropist whose charitableness knows no bounds.

Having never seen a Newman film (or many other films, for that matter), I met Paul Newman in 1999 after being recruited by Heidrick & Struggles to lead a nonprofit organization of CEOs committed to raising the level and quality of corporate philanthropy.

Paul, John Whitehead, and Peter Malkin spearheaded the founding of the Committee Encouraging Corporate Philanthropy (now called CECP), which was launched on November 18, 1999, with the *Wall Street Journal* headline: "Paul Newman Seeks Charity from CEOs."

In my first meeting with Paul, he confided that he wasn't really comfortable around CEOs and definitely didn't want to chair the organization alone. That led me to draft Ken Derr, who had just stepped down as CEO and chair of Chevron Corporation, to serve as cochair with Paul, which he did until 2004.

The Newman-Derr team was great as the two men complemented each other's skills. I usually met with Paul on the ground floor of his Manhattan apartment that was filled with movie posters featuring Paul and his wife, Joanne Woodward.

Paul liked to discuss fitness training and took great delight in comparing his daily four-hour workout with my paltry one-hour-twice-a-week routine. To make his point, he would take me to three or four closets full of Rube Goldberg exercise equipment to give demonstrations of what I was missing and then he would insist I take some of his equipment home with me.

He also insisted that he would stay only in hotels with six or more open flights of stairs so he could do wind sprints! When I challenged him on this, his assistant chimed in, "Trust him, Charlie, I travel with him and have to run those damn stairs, too!"

During our wide-ranging conversations, never without Fig Newman cookies, Paul always found time for my business agenda. In addition to attending our quarterly board meetings, Paul also agreed to participate in special CECP meetings.

When fellow Olympian Jim Wolfensohn (an Australian fencer) was chairman of the World Bank, he invited me to bring ten CECP CEOs to Washington to meet with ten World Bank leaders to discuss social issues.

The daylong event, which included an over-the-top formal luncheon, proved very successful. The icing on the cake came when Jim's executive assistant took me aside to request a special photograph of Paul with three floors' worth of secretaries! Paul obliged with charm. I'm betting that this group photo still hangs at the World Bank headquarters.

During Sandy Weill's tenure, we held our CECP director meetings following Citigroup's own board meetings. One day in 2006, Paul was early (not a usual occurrence), and he was very excited. As soon as the chair called our meeting to order, Paul interjected, "I have a new project for CECP, which will save the world!"

Paul introduced a water purifier invented by Dean Kamen that was effective enough to strip out arsenic and even purify urine. Given our mission to support and encourage the programs of our corporate members, we had to investigate this opportunity to help the one billion people in the world without access to clean water.

Fortunately, several CECP board members volunteered to organize and privately fund this project, which gave Paul what he wanted without compromising CECP's basic tenets. Within weeks, I joined this group to visit Kamen's lab in New Hampshire to better understand the proposed equipment.

On the negative side, it was heavy, expensive, and required electricity and meticulous maintenance, all real problems in remote areas where clean water is most needed. On the positive side, it worked. Kamen was invited to join the board of the Safe Water Network. In short order, the equipment and Kamen were dropped, but the vision survived.

Today, SWN excels at advancing market-based, affordable, safe, and reliable solutions for people who lack clean water. They are building local capacity through comprehensive training in areas that lack the technical and operational skills to manage and operate safe water stations in India and Ghana. In 2016, they provided access to safe water to 800,000 individuals. John Whitehead and Josh Weston, the former chairman and CEO of ADP, agreed to cochair SWN, and Josh continues in that role since John's passing.

In 2003 we combined our CECP Excellence in Corporate Philanthropy award ceremonies with Paul's run playing the role of the stage manager in a Broadway revival of Thornton Wilder's *Our Town*. The winners that year were Target and Whole Foods, but Newman stole the show.

At a special CECP directors' dinner in 2004 that was held to thank our initial cochairs and welcome Sandy Weill as new chair, Paul showed up with presents for the men: baseball caps emblazoned with OLD MEN RULE. I still wear mine!

It can be said that Paul Newman was a man of great gifts. At the same time, he was genuinely humble, believing in work, family, community, and the greater good. His hope for CECP was clear when Newman declared, "I helped to start CECP with the belief that corporate America could be a force for good in society."

Hear, hear!

The Duke of Edinburgh and
Other Brushes with Royalty

When I first met Prince Philip at the Olympics in 1952, I was humbled by my chance encounter with the spouse of the brand-new British queen. Over the years, I have had several opportunities to be in touch with him and his three sons.

Several days after settling into our Olympic Village in Helsinki, I joined a few Brits whom I had met as part of Cornell's exchange with Oxford and Cambridge in 1950. We sat down to dinner in the multipurpose mess hall that was designed and staffed to accommodate the different tastes of people all over the world.

Suddenly, we were confronted by a tall, distinguished man who greeted us with, "I say, may I join you chaps for dinner?" While I didn't recognize our visitor, my British friends did; and they responded, "It would be our honor, Your Royal

Highness." So the Duke of Edinburgh joined us for dinner.

Fast-forward to around 2005 when Judith and I had been invited to a gala dinner in London by the CEO of the International Business Leaders Forum, one of Prince Charles's charities.

After a long cocktail hour, we were ushered upstairs to the dining room. While waiting for the rest of the guests to assemble, I noticed that Prince Charles was standing alone at an adjacent table. Forgetting that you never shake hands with royalty until you are formally introduced, I popped over, held out my hand, and said, "I'm Charlie Moore, and I had dinner with your father in Helsinki in 1952." To which Prince Charles responded, "Very good; have you seen him since?"

That led to a polite conversation, and I found His Royal Highness to be very friendly but not nearly as outgoing as Camilla, Duchess of Cornwall, whom he married later that year.

Years later, as a commissioner of the Smithsonian National Postal Museum, I had the pleasure of meeting Prince Andrew, Duke of York, who was accompanying the Queen's magnificent stamp collection on its first trip to the United States. And, of course, I had the same conversation with Prince Andrew.

To complete my trifecta of royalty, I met Prince Edward, Earl of Wessex, at the 2009 memorial service for a dear friend who was related to Sophie, Countess of Wessex, and I had the same conversation with Prince Philip's youngest son.

When I shared this story with the eleventh rector of Saint Thomas Church Fifth Avenue, John Andrew, he insisted that I write to the Duke of Edinburgh and remind him of our "dinner with the boys in 1952" and tell him of the subsequent meetings with his sons.

With some hesitation, I did share my story with Prince Philip in a letter dated March 23. He wrote back in a letter mailed from Windsor Castle on March 28.

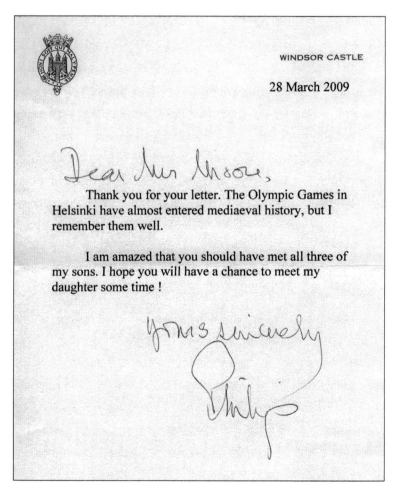

WINDSOR CASTLE

28 March 2009

Dear Mr Mason,

Thank you for your letter. The Olympic Games in Helsinki have almost entered mediaeval history, but I remember them well.

I am amazed that you should have met all three of my sons. I hope you will have a chance to meet my daughter some time !

Yours sincerely

Philip

Prince Philip's reply to my letter of March 23, 2009.

Roger Bannister

My initial encounters with the unforgettable Roger Bannister on the running tracks at Princeton and White City Stadium have flourished into a lifetime friendship with Roger and his wife, Moyra.

Roger represented Great Britain in the Olympic 1,500 meters in Helsinki in 1952 in a race that was up for grabs. If there were favorites, they were probably Werner Lueg, who had just tied the world record at the German championships on June 29, and Roger, whose greatest fame was yet to come.

Bannister, a medical intern, had prepared very carefully for a competition that would include a heat and then a final two days later. But IAFF officials decided to add a semifinal round, which meant that the finalists would run three races in three days (certainly more difficult than my own two races per day over two days in the 400-meter hurdles).

The final was a great race with six of the twelve finalists achieving their personal-best time. Bannister was fifth at 3:46.0, but his "day" was getting closer.

Roger expected that the summer of 1954 would be his last competitive season, but it was certain to be a big year as hopes were running high for a four-minute mile.

And these hopes were realized on May 6, 1954, when Bannister became the first person to run a mile in under four minutes. But Bannister's record was broken by Australian John Landy on June 2. Then on August 7 the stage was set in Vancouver: Landy versus Bannister in the British Empire and Commonwealth Games. It was another great effort on the part of both athletes, with Bannister winning in 3:58.8 and finishing five yards ahead of Landy.

But Roger Bannister is far more than a celebrated athlete; he is also a distinguished neurologist and one of his nation's best-loved public figures. He conducted outpatient clinics and rounds at both the National Hospital and St. Mary's twice a week while he did research, gave lectures, and published medical papers and books.

Following his own athletic career, Bannister's interest in sports in Britain remained undiminished. This was partly out of his wanting to promote good health and partly to share the pleasure sports can bring to participants. In time, Roger served as chairman of the Sports Council. He retired after serving ten years in 1974, and was knighted in 1975. He then returned to Oxford and was appointed Master of Pembroke College.

In retirement, heeding Churchill's advice that a man should do something with his hands, his brain, and his body, Bannister joined a wood-carving class, started a book club, and organized a walking club.

Roger graciously wrote the foreword for the forthcoming book I'm championing that chronicles the transformative experiences of Cornell track athletes in the exchange with Oxford and Cambridge.[2]

In 2014 Roger, inspired by the role that sports and medicine have in improving people's lives, wrote his autobiography, *Twin Tracks*. In Judith's and my copy, he noted, "With fond

---

2 *Lift the Chorus, Speed It Onward: A Celebration of 100 Years of Cornell Track and Field and the TransAtlantic Series.*

Roger Bannister (left) and I at the 2011 Oxford Analytica Conference.

memories of our joint athletic past. In memory of 1949–2014: over 65 years!"

Several years ago, I was attending an Oxford Analytica Conference in Oxford, and officials invited Roger and me and our wives to sit at the high table. When we were introduced, nearly 300 people rose and applauded for more than fifteen minutes. This says volumes about the life of Sir Roger Bannister and the respect the world still has for him.

TREASURED EXPERIENCES

My First Presidential Encounter

My first visit to the White House was hosted by President Eisenhower in 1953. The president and first lady invited nearly fifty "name" athletes from all sports, including Joe Louis, Joe DiMaggio, and many of my other boyhood heroes.

What impressed me the most was Ike's genuine interest

With President Eisenhower at the White House, and the invitation that brought me there.

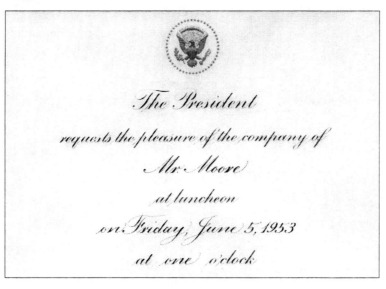

in each athlete and their records. Although I wasn't sure I quite belonged there, I was incredibly honored that my hard work and dedication to my sport garnered the attention of the president of the United States.

My Second Presidential Encounter

During the time I served as a public sector director of the USOC and chair of its audit committee, President and Mrs. Clinton hosted several events to recognize the USOC and its Olympic athletes. The president and first lady were always gracious and enthusiastic in welcoming Olympians into their residence.

In 2005 Judith and I joined Senator Clinton to represent the U.S. in Singapore when the IOC was choosing the city to host the 2012 Summer Games. Mrs. Clinton was an enthusiastic supporter of the New York bid to bring the Games back to the U.S.

I have also been a guest multiple times at the president's prestigious Clinton Global Initiative, through which he has made a real difference in the lives of people around the world, and he graciously spoke at one of my CECP summits.

My Third Presidential Encounter

From 2000 to 2008, I had the honor to serve on President Bush's President's Council on Physical Fitness and Sports, which led to multiple visits to the White House.

The CEO of Trek Bicycle, John Burke, chaired the council during my second term, which led to several serious bicycling workouts with number 43. He can really go!

More subdued but equally exciting was the time Judith and I were invited to the White House by the Bushes for dinner and a screening of *Seabiscuit*. It was very cool sitting in the private theater with Laura Hillenbrand, the book's author; several of the actors from the movie; our friends the producers Kathleen Kennedy and Frank Marshall; and, of course, Steven Spielberg. But I couldn't tell whether the president fell asleep or not! He had been traveling all day, and the presidential chopper had just dropped him off on the White House lawn!

THE OLYMPIC BID CITY CIRCUIT

As a result of George Steinbrenner's connection and encouragement, I served as the chair of the United States Olympic Committee's bid city task force. Our mission was to reduce the eight cities that had been nominated to the two that the board of directors would choose to represent the United States in 2012.

Our competition that year was with four other finalists: London, Paris, Madrid, and Moscow.

We adopted the IOC's procedures to assess competition facilities; transportation networks; environmental issues; airports, hotels, and restaurants; security; the reuse of facilities after the Games; and projected costs. We also added our own subjective assessment of how attractive the city would appear to the more than one hundred visiting IOC delegates.

We were operating in the aftermath of the Salt Lake City

bribery scandals, so there was a new protocol for what our host cities could or could not do for us.

And that was not the only external pressure! The September 11, 2001, terrorist attacks on New York and Washington had to be addressed. Out of sympathy, the mayor of Rome offered to withdraw his city's bid for the 2012 Games if the USOC picked New York as its candidate city.

The newly installed IOC president, Jacques Rogge, eschewed this proposal by saying, "We must complete the bid process to ensure that the athletes get the most qualified host. New York must win on its own merit, not because of sympathy or condolences." He was right, of course.

We started with eight cities that were going for the gold with strong community, business, and government support, and that were prepared to invest up to $20 million in this exploration. In the first go-round, my team visited Washington, Dallas, Houston, Cincinnati, New York, Tampa, San Francisco, and Los Angeles to inspect their facilities, some only in the planning stages.

Our evaluation team was terrific. It included the former mayor of Salt Lake City, the retired superintendent of the Denver public school system, several athlete representatives, several National Governing Body representatives, Roland Betts (another public sector director), and USOC staffers (including Greg Harney, who was indispensable).

As chair, I concluded each visit with a press conference, where the reporters were only interested in how their city stacked up with the rest even if we hadn't visited all of the cities yet!

In Dallas, I was awarded a "gold medal" for "ambiguity, concealment, elusiveness, evasiveness, obfuscation and all-around vagueness!"

I made some mistakes, as well, such as referring to Euless (a town we visited outside Dallas that was the proposed site for softball) as "Useless." In the same session, I was asked what I thought of the weather. Without hesitation, I truthfully reported, "It's hot."

I also conducted private sessions with each city's organizing group where we shared valuable information on how the city could improve its bid. Throughout the process, I was always sensitive to the fact that I lived in Washington and worked in New York.

As part of our inspection of Tampa, we had lunch with Governor Jeb Bush in Orlando, where the city's committee proposed to hold certain competitions. When I inquired how they were going to shuttle athletes, officials, and spectators back and forth between the two cities, Governor Bush looked me straight in the eye and said that if they got the bid, he would guarantee me that he would build a high-speed train between Tampa and Orlando. I believe he would have!

After a careful review of all eight voluminous bid books and surveying the projected grounds and facilities, we were ready to reduce the numbers.

The result? Dallas, Cincinnati, Tampa, and Los Angeles were dropped, the latter being the most controversial. After all, Los Angeles was the only city that had any experience in hosting the Games—in 1932 and in 1984, the latter event probably being the most successful Olympics ever!

184 • RUNNING ON PURPOSE

So what goes? Among other things, Los Angeles refused to meet the IOC requirement of a financial guarantee. They hadn't done that before, and they thought the IOC was bluffing! We couldn't run that risk. I even consulted with the governor of California when I realized that San Francisco faced the same challenge, as did all the other cities around the world that were bidding.

After revisiting the four remaining cities and answering countless questions from the organizing committees and the press, ten of us spent seven hours in a Chicago airport hotel on August 28, 2002. Frankly, it wasn't pretty; we were deadlocked for the first time, particularly around Washington, San Francisco, and New York.

It's hard to believe, but reporters were listening through transoms and challenging our security to get the scoop on our decision. It was even less pretty when I had to announce that the task force would recommend New York and San Francisco!

The *Washington Post* "reported" our vote tally as New York nine, San Francisco six, Washington five, and Houston zero even though our task force released no such scoring. To make matters worse, we were accused of going with our "gut feeling" according to the *Post*.

Despite the *Post's* unfounded reporting and allegations, I reported in the concluding press conference that "we felt San Francisco and New York were infinitesimally more electable than Washington. We had to pick a great technical bid. We also had to pick someone that would get elected by the IOC. We had a lot of discussion about that!"

On November 2, 2002, the USOC board of directors met in Colorado Springs to select the city that would represent the U.S. in the competition to host the 2012 Summer Olympics. Everyone was tense, especially me. Lobbyists were everywhere. There was no clear favorite.

Despite some last-minute squabbling and delays, I introduced the finalists, who made their "hearts and minds" pitches with professional and dramatic style. The chair called for the vote. New York won with 59 percent of the weighted vote, and my job was over!

In 2005 we were invited to go to Singapore for the IOC voting, and we lost to London on the second ballot. Would a different U.S. city have won? I don't think so. Now we must wait until at least 2024 for the Summer Games to return to our shores. Incidentally, Mayor Bloomberg, Senator Clinton, and other New York luminaries convened for the final cocktail reception and were very gracious even though they were disappointed in the loss of the Games.

Fortunately, Judith and I didn't have to wait that long to reenergize our Olympic passion. We went to Sydney in 2000 and London in 2012 (the Games for which New York had competed).

Long live the Olympic spirit!

Chapter 11

DRIVING CORPORATE
CHARITY TO IMPACT

*Wealth is not new. Neither is charity. But the idea of using
private wealth imaginatively, constructively, and systematically
to attack the fundamental problems of mankind is new.*

—JOHN W. GARDNER, FORMER SECRETARY OF
HEALTH, EDUCATION, AND WELFARE

*The highest use of capital is not to make more money but to
make money to do more for the betterment of life.*

—HENRY FORD

THE CALL THAT CHANGED IT ALL

In the summer of 1999, I received a phone call that would
change the trajectory of the rest of my life.

I was sitting in my office at Cornell when a recruiter from

Heidrick & Struggles pitched the notion that I should become the founding executive director of a small nonprofit that had heavyweight support from the business community.

At the time, it was little more than a very big idea in the minds of a handful of corporate luminaries, but I was intrigued when I learned that their vision was to raise the level and quality of corporate philanthropy.

My interest was heightened further when I learned that the leaders advancing this philosophy were men I had long admired: John C. Whitehead, Peter Malkin, and Paul Newman. And they were being bolstered by honorary support from David Rockefeller and Paul Volcker.

The founders of CECP (from left to right), John Whitehead, Paul Newman, and Peter Malkin in 1999.

Despite the fact that there was no business plan and no long-term funding—and that I would need to live out of a hotel room in the Cornell Club for what would turn out to be more than two years—I said yes to this opportunity.

Throughout my career, I never planned to stay at any one company or institution for too long. I define myself as a change agent—the one to call when energetic decision making is needed at a pivotal moment.

Nonetheless, I remained at the helm of CECP for thirteen years—my longest tenure at any organization except my family business—and my course since then has been influenced by the ideas that were at the center of our work there.

What kept my interest and passion so high for so long was the central issue at stake. I would soon discover that something even more essential than raising the level and quality of corporate giving was at our mission's heart: We needed to define the "right" role of business in society.

THE NEED FOR CECP

Given how much the world has changed since 1999, it's almost quaint to reflect on the general public's expectations of business before the new millennium.

In fact, it's easy for me and my contemporaries to recall an even earlier time when CEOs lived in the same neighborhoods as the managers and employees who worked alongside them. Unlike the ruthlessly successful industrialists of the late nineteenth century, most corporate leaders from my era didn't have houses in every chic capital of the world; instead, they led modestly by today's standards. While it's a cliché, it was indeed a simpler time.

The public's respect for CEOs in those days was much higher than it is now. Business was trusted, and CEOs were civic leaders and community ambassadors.

By 1999, things were already starting to change, and CECP's founders were clearly responding to that change. Business was becoming more global, more optimized, and more spreadsheet driven. Maximizing returns to shareholders was becoming scientific, and delivering results quarter after quarter was becoming a blood sport.

What the founders of CECP realized very early on was that corporate success and community success could not be thought of as separate. Instead, they needed to be recognized as being intertwined. While it's true that a company might thrive independently of the health of the surrounding community, it will eventually need the people and services that surround it to be successful also if it hopes to grow.

It was just as this thinking was starting to coalesce that I took the job at CECP.

THE LEGEND OF PAUL NEWMAN

Funding in those early days was from a handful of visionary public foundations, most notably the Ford Foundation.

CECP founder Peter Malkin needs little prompting to share one of his favorite memories from those early days. He had asked Paul Newman to join him in an important meeting with Susan Berresford, the president of the Ford Foundation.

Susan joined Ford in 1970 as a project assistant and her talents carried her to the top role in 1996.

When Peter and Paul walked through the hushed hallways toward Susan's office, they created a wake of fans and admirers all along their route. The success of the meeting exceeded all hopes when Peter and Paul shook hands with Susan for a commitment of $250,000, support that Ford sustained for four years.

As he exited the building, Paul remarked to Peter, lowering his glasses to let his famous blue eyes shine, "Seventy-five years old and still sexy!"

It's worth noting that Paul, along with everything else he did for CECP, pledged $125,000 in annual support for four years.

OVERCOMING FEARS

CECP started with ten vice chairmen. Despite that bench strength, none of the ten was willing to step forward to serve as CECP's first chairman of the board. Paul Newman would have been an excellent choice given his fame, credibility, and personal passion, but he, too, demurred. This was when I persuaded Ken Derr and Paul to team up, and they served brilliantly until 2004.

Those earliest days would be recognizable to any entrepreneur in the late 1990s. CECP was a start-up, which made every use of our time and financial resources a weighty decision.

My partner in defining and building a functional coalition was Suzanne Brose. In order to share CECP's bold vision, I was on the phone from early morning to late at night, navigating my way past the legions of handlers who regulate access to their company's CEO. I sought personal commitments to not only invest in communities philanthropically but also to prove that giving back to the community was an investment in future business health.

But in those days, the vision of CECP ran counter to the famous Milton Friedman quote: "The business of business is business." And I needed to overcome some prevailing fears that CEOs expressed in those early conversations. They were afraid that their stockholders would accuse them of abandoning their fiduciary responsibility by giving money away and that the general public would be cynical about their motives for interfering with public services.

My most successful mantra that brought CEOs over to CECP's way of thinking was the concept of "the license to operate."

The central notion is that business is granted a "license to operate" by the community in which it works, and if it doesn't step up to the public's expectations of community engagement, it risks the public's revocation of that license.

From 1999 to 2004, we went from a handful of CEOs to more than ninety engaged CEOs; today, active membership is approaching 150.

TAKING ON BIG ISSUES RIGHT
OUT OF THE GATE

My first priority at CECP's helm was to make sure we were getting out of the station on the right track. I disagreed early and vigorously with our founders on a crucial point: Would a corporation who agreed with CECP's mission be required to give a fixed percentage of the company's profits to charity?

The idea of a mandatory giving minimum as a percentage of corporate profits had taken hold very firmly in some circles. The most famous of these is Minnesota's Five Percent Club, founded in 1976 by twenty-three companies that agreed to give 5 percent of their profits to charity.

But despite the success of this group and its many imitators, my instincts as a former CEO told me that this would be very limiting if applied to CECP's nascent membership. For starters, CEOs don't like to be told what to do with their company's profits! Also, given the quickening rate of CEO turnover, I knew that even if we managed to compel a CEO to sign on to a percentage-of-profit commitment we'd surely be at risk if his or her successor abandoned our cause given the pressures facing any CEO new to the job.

The CECP board soon agreed with my logic.

THE NEXT WAVE OF GROWTH

In 2004 Sandy Weill took the reins of CECP's board. Sandy, who had been named by *Financial World* magazine as CEO of the Year in 1998 and received the same honor from *Chief Executive* magazine in 2002, was an incredible asset to me in supercharging CECP's next wave of growth.

Sandy was one of the earliest "rock star" CEOs, and his passion for giving back was infamous. It helped all the more that Sandy and I were fellow Cornellians and had developed our rapport during my days as athletic director. It also helped that Ken Derr was a Cornellian and served on Sandy's Citigroup board. Small world!

AWARDING EXCELLENCE

As our roster of CEOs grew, so did our team and suite of offerings. Cari Hills, whom I had known when she was an exemplary undergraduate scholar athlete at Cornell, came aboard in 2003 from Accenture to serve as CECP's chief operating officer.

In addition to Cari's organizing five CEOs and their companies to offer a sustainable response to the areas in Pakistan hit hardest by the devastating earthquake of 2005, we initiated CECP's Excellence Awards and Corporate Philanthropy Day to celebrate companies that demonstrated CEO leadership and a commitment to measurement, innovation, and partnership.

After the first three Excellence Awards ceremonies, we required the winners to accept the award in person, and I remember vividly the speech Pfizer CEO Hank McKinnell gave in 2004 when he told story after story about Pfizer's commitment to its communities that went back to the company's founding. He set the bar high for the many CEOs who followed him.

Awards were given each year to a large company, a smaller company, and a nonprofit; the response was always the same: thrilled and honored!

Our closed-door, CEO-only awards ceremony became

the prototype for an event that would come to be recognized as among the world's top executive gatherings by the PR firm Weber Shandwick. Using the Clinton Global Initiative and the World Economic Forum series in Davos as models, CECP launched its first Board of Boards conference in 2006, which was attended by twenty-eight CEOs and chairpersons.

Leaders such as John Chambers, president and CEO of Cisco; Bill Harrison, chairman of JPMorgan Chase; and Bob Nardelli, chairman, president, and CEO of The Home Depot, came together on such themes as the need for greater transparency surrounding corporate giving, best practices in collaboration, and the most effective ways to create societal impact.

CHARLIE ROSE

Over the years, the Board of Boards series has attracted more than 200 different CEOs with such important themes as The CEO's Challenge: Leading the Company, Shaping Society, and Next Generation Community Involvement. These conversations were enlivened by live audience polling and the expert moderation of journalistic luminaries whose expertise in driving straight to the heart of an issue elicited insights from our audience that triggered CEOs to return to their offices and make important changes—and allowed CECP to share lessons with their peers year-round.

Of all of our esteemed moderators, Charlie Rose stands out in my memory as a favorite, especially since I had long been a regular viewer of his show on PBS. After I was introduced to him, I have gotten to know him even better and respect him even more.

I do have vivid memories of our February 2009 conference, our first since the fall of Bear Stearns and Lehman Brothers and the sudden free fall of the global financial markets in late 2008. Our theme in that year was Global Leaders: Confronting a Crucial Decision, and despite the lingering chaos and uncertainty in the markets, we attracted fifty-five CEOs to our roundtable, which was anchored by Jeffrey Immelt of GE, Carlos Ghosn of Nissan, and Tom Brokaw of NBC News. Their presence proved that corporate philanthropy is a business priority even in a strained economic climate.

In 2010 CECP boldly hosted two Board of Boards conferences in the same year. One was held in New York City and led by ABC News correspondent Chris Bury. Just a few months later, we met in May with the support of KPMG's Michael Hastings and the financial services firm Bloomberg L.P.

CECP hosted its first and only international event in London. The event could not have been held in a more exciting place nor at a more exciting time. The Board of Boards coincided with the United Kingdom's general election, and CECP was honored to host a dinner at the Houses of Parliament as the historic election results were being tallied. It was a tremendous feeling to walk through corridors drenched in history on that historic night surrounded by like-minded business leaders from across Europe.

For every Board of Boards conference, the Empire State

Building was lit in CECP's colors of blue and green, and CECP rang the NYSE opening or closing bell. My preference was always to ring the opening bell so that CECP would not be associated with any day's losses!

EXPANDING OUR RELATIONSHIPS AND OFFERINGS

By this time, our offerings for corporate giving officers had dramatically expanded.

In CECP's earliest days, we had trained our sights on working directly with CEOs, but over time, we also built relationships with terrific individuals on the front lines of global societal change. While their job titles varied widely, their essential job responsibilities were the same: overseeing the philanthropic giving, volunteer efforts, and overall corporate social responsibility of their firms.

We affectionately called this group our Chief Giving Officers despite the fact that their roles went far beyond charitable giving.

THE CORPORATE GIVING STANDARD

In 2000 CECP decided to collect and analyze corporate contributions data from our cohort of companies so they could benchmark their generosity against their relevant peers. We called this effort the Corporate Giving Standard.

Seventeen companies participated in our benchmarking survey that first year. Growing this initiative required developing a set of valuation standards that could be applied consistently across companies from every sector and then creating an incentive to participate.

Margaret Coady (now executive director of corporate social responsibility for Coach Inc.) joined the CECP family in 2005 and was tasked with growing the participation base and transitioning our tool to a fee-based structure. At my urging, she created an advisory committee comprised of our early adopters, and after just a single meeting of this group, Margaret had a long to-do list. Foremost on her list was building confidence in the accuracy of the data and the desirability of the peer set.

A narrow focus on building adoptions among Fortune 100 companies and Coady's creation of our landmark *Giving in Numbers* reports—as well as her sharing the insights from this one-of-a-kind data with corporations all over the world—quickly transformed a little-known survey into the definitive record of why and how corporate giving was changing over time.

The database and accompanying reports quickly differentiated CECP among our companies and became a primary method for raising the level and quality of giving. In some instances, equipping a company with the right benchmarking data led to a doubling or tripling of their charitable giving.

It was very satisfying for Margaret and the team to see the changes that resulted from their efforts to enable corporate giving officers to speak the language of business and advocate for increased corporate generosity and community engagement.

THE CORPORATE PHILANTHROPY SUMMIT

The results of each year's survey were shared at our Corporate Philanthropy Summit. The Summit began as a half-day affair that featured outside speakers and CGOs. In just a few short years, the expectation that CECP staff would step into the limelight as experts in the field caused us to take hold of the event with both hands and run it to its full potential.

Over the years, Cari Hills, Lindsay Siegel, Margaret Coady, and Courtney Murphy took turns growing the conference to a two-day must-attend event for senior leaders in corporate social responsibility. Seating was limited, and companies were telling us that there were internal competitions about who got to attend. Our audience of 250 of the top leaders in corporate giving, who gave a total of more than $12 billion annually, made it possible for us to attract any speaker we wanted. Who would turn down a chance to influence the giving of so many?

Katie Couric of *The Today Show* interviewed tennis champion Andre Agassi about his charity work in Las Vegas; General Colin L. Powell discussed the link between high school graduation rates and national security; U.N. Ambassador Richard Holbrooke shared urgent needs in global health; *Huffington Post* Editor in Chief Arianna Huffington highlighted the relationships that form the heart of social media and urged greater collaboration; and Mayor Cory Booker of Newark, New Jersey, discussed the importance of public-private partnerships and corporate investment in cities.

BILL CLINTON

One summit highlight for me was the last-minute acceptance by President Bill Clinton to address our audience in 2008.

I had been networking to advance our invitation with the former president for months, but the schedules of world leaders are understandably difficult to pin down. Our CECP team was elated to get the call that President Clinton was able to join us even though it came twenty-four hours before the summit and there were no open slots remaining!

We sent a notice to all conference attendees that the summit would start earlier than planned because of our surprise

Presenting President Bill Clinton at the 2008 CECP Summit.

guest—and we opened our breakfast program early. Adding to the usual chaos of hosting the summit was the fact that President Clinton's equally famous wife was on the verge of dropping out of her primary race against Barack Obama. Anticipating that Bill Clinton might drop a hint about Hillary's intentions, every media outlet suddenly wanted to cover CECP's philanthropy conference.

The back wall of the plenary conference room was lined floor to ceiling with media crews and paparazzi. We even had to create a media overflow room to accommodate all of the interest. In a scramble, I had to make do with the Wikipedia entry on President Clinton for my introduction as there wasn't sufficient time to thoroughly prepare. His remarks were a tremendous success, and we will always be grateful to have had the chance to share his thoughts with our assembly of corporate leaders.

PARTNERING WITH AMERICANS FOR THE ARTS

In addition to providing thought-provoking speakers and networking opportunities, CECP partnered with Americans for the Arts to include arts programming in the summits. One of my favorite pieces was an excerpt of the play *ReEntry*, created by Emily Ackerman and KJ Sanchez of the American Records theater company.

This documentary-theater work is based on transcripts of interviews with Marines returning from war. Our audience, including me, was transfixed by the simply staged performance that let the raw words of our heroes motivate us to better serve our veterans in their return to civilian life.

Moments like these, combined with my service as a national board member of the Smithsonian Institution, remind me of the underacknowledged role of the arts in today's conversations on philanthropy and social investing.

SUSTAINABLE VALUE CREATION

On CECP's ten-year anniversary, Margaret Coady and I embarked on a listening tour with some of the greatest thinkers in our field to figure out what the future might hold in the decade ahead.

I remember fondly a breakfast with Diana Aviv, CEO of Independent Sector, where she shared the influential work her organization was undertaking to answer the same question. It was a meeting with Lenny Mendonca of McKinsey & Company, a great futurist as well as McKinsey's top social-innovation expert, that caused CECP to embark on a path of groundbreaking research that began under the five-year chairmanship of Terry McGraw, the CEO of the McGraw-Hill Companies.

CECP's thought-leadership publications were based on interviews with our leading CEO members. CECP published *Shaping the Future: Solving Social Problems Through Business Strategy* in partnership with top-flight economists and consultants from McKinsey & Company who worked pro bono. In this report, we coined the term "sustainable value creation" and outlined the forces that were fundamentally changing the playing field for capitalism: increasing scarcity of natural resources, shifting demographics, the shift in economic power from West to East, the interconnectedness of global markets, and the competition among nations to attract business.

The report also addressed society's rapidly rising expectations of business and the uncertainty about whether or not companies would step up to meet these higher expectations. The possible corporate responses to all of these changes led to the conclusion that sustainable value creation was the best course for business and served to strengthen my own conviction that this was the real purpose of all corporations.

CECP followed this report in 2011 with *Business at Its Best: Driving Sustainable Value Creation*, written in partnership with an excellent team of consultants from Accenture, that offers a practical roadmap for companies to apply a sustainable value creation approach.

Through a generous fellowship program with Goldman Sachs, CECP also published *Measuring the Value of Corporate Philanthropy*, in which Terence Lim outlines a practical framework for quantifying the impact of corporate grants and societal investment.

Many of these publications were ahead of their time and continue to be downloaded frequently by nonprofit leaders, academics, government officials, and corporate leaders.

DOUG CONANT AT THE HELM

As our reputation and impact grew, CECP was blessed with another excellent and engaged chairman: Doug Conant, the former CEO of the Campbell Soup Company, coauthor of the book *TouchPoints: Creating Powerful Leadership Connections in the Smallest of Moments*, and chair of the Kellogg Executive Leadership Institute.

Doug presided over a refresh of CECP's strategic plan and our rebranding efforts led by FutureBrand and James Cockerille, which clarified and extended CECP's core values. Under Doug's leadership, we also expanded the roster of top female executives on CECP's board. At a time when low female presence on boards is rightly lamented, CECP is fortunate to have Shelly Lazarus, Marilyn Carlson Nelson, Henrietta Holsman Fore, Deanna Mulligan, and Sheri McCoy fully engaged in leading its governance.

A STORMY SEND-OFF

One last adventure awaited me as I began to prepare for my retirement from CECP: Superstorm Sandy.

In October of 2012 it was business as usual at CECP. We had just published the latest edition of *Giving in Numbers* and were preparing for our upcoming CEO conference when Hurricane Sandy struck New York City and deposited more than thirty feet of seawater in the basement of our office building at 110 Wall Street. While our offices were not submerged, the electrical and safety systems of our office building were destroyed.

In the immediate aftermath of the storm, we had optimistically assumed that we would be allowed to return to our offices within a few weeks. After I visited Lower Manhattan to speak to the building manager and assess the damages, it was clear that returning was a folly. Our office building would be out of commission indefinitely. At the same time, several CECP colleagues were personally affected by the storm, with one staffer having to race from her one-story home on the Jersey shore in the middle of the night for the safety of a neighbor's two-story house. Most of her possessions were damaged or lost; yet she was the one to lead CECP's move to a new location over the holidays.

I spent the Christmas holiday of 2012 working with lawyers and realtors to secure a new space and begin construction work so our team could move in. In the interim, our friends at the Conference Board in Midtown accommodated us for more than three months as we prepared our new home. This was one last burst of excitement before I would turn leadership of CECP over to Daryl Brewster (who was appointed CEO) and Margaret Coady in February 2013.

CHERISHED GOOD-BYES

The farewells that greeted me as I prepared for a new chapter were overwhelming. Jeff Immelt of GE, Klaus Kleinfeld of Alcoa, Jean-Pierre Garnier of GlaxoSmithKline, Lloyd Blankfein of Goldman Sachs, Barry Salzberg of Deloitte, Marc Benioff of Salesforce, and many others paused their important work to share a kind word, for which I will be forever grateful. My most cherished quotes about my departure include:

Over the past thirteen years, you have taken a dream of others and made it a reality for so many. The Olympic flame still burns brightly in you. Thank you for touching us all with that same spirit.

Charlie is the rarest of leaders in that he is 100 percent conviction and clarity, and he is vividly passionate about getting things done right and first.

You have transformed a nascent organization that few people knew about into the voice of corporate philanthropy. You have helped evolve the concept of corporate social responsibility to a central place in corporate strategy and governance and done so in your classy, self-effacing style. With many people clamoring for the time and commitment of CEOs, you have been the one it was very difficult to say no to—in fact, you would never take no for an answer.

Without your persistence, dedication, and, let's face it, refusal to take no for an answer, it would have been impossible for CECP to have accomplished all that it has. You have transformed the organization into an invaluable partner for the business community.

Under your leadership, CECP has championed a powerful, positive vision of the highest and best role business can play in society.

Charlie, I will forever be grateful to have had the
opportunity to work under your leadership. Your vision,
dedication, encouragement, and warmth put you in a
unique category of "best" bosses. The best part is that
I know I am only one of hundreds, if not thousands
of people personally inspired by you in the course of
your illustrious career.

Leaving aside the personal accolades, these comments provide an important perspective on CECP's journey. The CECP staff was the best part: bright, energized, young, competitive, completely committed, and mostly female. The crazy part is that with all the fun we had and with all that we accomplished we ran CECP like a financially successful business.

DRIVING CHANGE FROM
CHARITY TO IMPACT

I am not sure that business will ever invest enough in their communities—there is always more to do. However, I am extremely proud of the role CECP has played and continues to play in corporate philanthropy.

Thanks to CECP and inspired CEO leadership, corporations now believe that their social investments are a core business strategy. They find that they are most effective when they bring the best of their business to their corporate philanthropy as they seek a higher purpose and prioritize societal need while driving business performance.

I relished witnessing and being a catalyst for this change

in mindset. Most of all, I loved meeting with CEOs, not just because it was critical to build an engaged, diverse membership but because I was privileged to see firsthand what the world's leading executives could do to help solve the world's greatest challenges.

Chapter 12

MY CALL TO ACTION: THE LICENSE TO LEAD

The strategy to achieve a company's purpose should reflect the values and culture of the company and should not be developed in isolation. Boards should oversee both.

—SIR WINFRIED BISCHOFF, FORMER
CHAIRMAN OF LLOYDS BANKING GROUP

TAKING STOCK

Up to now, I have shared with you my experiences and be-havior in terms of purpose, which I believe has shaped and driven me both as an individual and a team player.

Purpose has been profoundly important because it has given me a level of alignment with myself and others that was deeper than surface appearances and more authentic. Embracing a purpose is ultimately a human commitment.

The ability to meld our separate purposes into something shared is the greatest power we have as a species.

Now I want to share the culmination of my aspirations (and my dreams), which I see as my call to action. They are built on five premises but have only one outcome.

1. Businesses are not playing the game or following the rules we need them to.

2. The new game is one of sustainable value creation (SVC). It is one based on corporate purpose and is strategically deeper than financial valuation can measure.

3. As a new game, it requires a new and simple frame of reference that is shared by all players. We need to understand the combined effect of what a company deems material to its sustainable value equation and how results relate to those of other companies.

4. There is important groundwork available to help identify some of the fundamentals of sustainable value creation.

5. We must all do our part.

A successful outcome will result from the acceptance and execution of the second and third premises: *Long-term value creation must be at the center of everything.*

And I advocate a system that measures both economic and social values, and allows us to integrate these measurements of benefits into financial valuations and business decisions.

Are there constraints? Yes, I believe that long-term corporate success is most often constrained by three negative factors: short-term thinking, a lack of trust in business, and an insufficient focus on intangible assets.

CEOs are aware of these three constraints. Indeed, CEOs are among the most vocal in articulating them. However, they face real-world challenges that keep these constraints in place despite the desire on the part of many CEOs to measure and convincingly communicate their company's long-term value-creation story.

My call to action therefore envisions three must-haves:

1. A framework[3] to define and explain the purpose of the corporation and to "redefine corporate success for tomorrow's companies." The ideal SVC framework would help CEOs and their directors measure and convincingly communicate their value-creation story. This ideal framework should be specifically targeted to unlock the potential value of intangible assets.

---

3 For brevity, I use the term "framework" to indicate how a range of relevant concepts, issues, and measures could become a shared reference. My intent is not to suggest a technical model in which all variables for every business situation have been defined and preset. Such an outcome is perhaps too impractical and certainly beyond the scope of this book. Furthermore, there are already "frameworks" of this kind in play. Rather, I use the term "framework" in my call to action to suggest a way of merging a broad variety of factors into a single vocabulary that corporations, analysts, investors, individuals, and boards can use to advance the role and benefits of sustainable value creation. The emphasis is on sharing a new way of seeing the world and committing to the terms, proxies, practices, and benchmarks that make a more sustainable form of competition possible.

2. An opportunity to invest and participate in new research that is critical for present and future generations of businesses as they explore a new "license to lead." The related elements of the ideal SVC framework would be metrics, case studies, long-term statistical analysis, and a framework and vocabulary that can be customized for each company's circumstances.

3. An opportunity to focus business leadership around central themes and future contingencies that create sustainable value over the foreseeable future and establish a collective CEO voice. The research that would go into the ideal SVC framework should be built on and around productivity, innovation, and business strategies and models.

How value is defined here is the critical element because it works in two interrelated ways. On the one hand, value benefits the organization by providing financial returns to the providers of financial capital. On the other hand, there is the value that benefits stakeholders and society as a whole. The very art of business is to align these two to best effect. This happens through a wide range of activities, interactions, and relationships that involve more than those who are directly associated with changes in capital.

The complexity of the modern, globalized, hyperconnected market favors those companies that can understand and respond quickly to stakeholder concerns. Companies that engage in ongoing and productive dialogues with long-term stakeholders will gain insights that will allow them to integrate this information into their business strategy and gain a competitive advantage.

In today's world, companies can't create long-term shareholder value without managing sustainability factors, and *ecological* sustainability is only a part of this equation. But companies don't have to choose between profit and sustainable value. Our capital markets operate under the assumption that investors are economic actors who want the best return they can get for the risk they are taking, and ignoring sustainability heightens the risk for investors.

In my work at CECP, I interviewed hundreds of CEOs about sustainable value creation. While they didn't all see the same components as I did for SVC, they all agreed that the purpose of business is *sustainable value creation*. However, various members of corporate boards feel differently. A McKinsey study done in 2015 showed that more than 50 percent of directors believe that their number one priority is the financial results of the company, and very few of them identified long-term sustainable value creation as something that should be regularly discussed in board meetings.[4] At the same time, the demand is overwhelming from all constituencies (especially certain investor groups) for more oversight into how companies do business.

Technology, the emphasis on transparency, regulatory changes, the scarcity of natural resources, and changing

---

4 The study was done as part of the Focusing Capital on the Long Term initiative cosponsored by the Canada Pension Plan Investment Board and McKinsey & Company.

societal expectations are systemic trends that continue to drive the concept of SVC. Most of these raise issues of fiduciary duty on both the corporate (specifically company boards) and the investor side.

I want to single out four initiatives that should be recognized for laying the groundwork for better understanding sustainable value creation.

1. Michael Porter and Mark Kramer's shared value initiative relates to a management strategy that focuses on creating measurable business value by identifying and addressing social problems that intersect a company's business.[5]

2. The Sustainability Accounting Standards Board. Founded in 2011, SASB has developed sustainability accounting standards that help public corporations disclose information that is useful to investors.

3. The Global Reporting Initiative. GRI provides the world's most widely used standards on sustainability reporting and disclosure, which enable businesses, governments, and citizens to make better decisions on critical sustainability issues.

4. The International Integrated Reporting Council. IIRC was designed to enhance and consolidate existing reporting practices and compile information about an

---

5 See Porter and Kramer's "Creating Shared Value," *Harvard Business Review*, January–February 2011.

organization's strategy, governance, performance, and prospects in a way that reflects the commercial, social, and environmental context within which it operates.

Still, there is no consensus for how to measure the success and progress of SVC. And this is the missing link that keeps CEOs from countering the negative forces that hold businesses back. Although certainly not a movement, there is a growing commitment to explore how to engage my themes of *long-term thinking, trust in business,* and the *value of intangibles.* This is both a blessing and a curse. The Global Initiative for Sustainability Ratings tells us that there are about 120 rating agencies that offer more than 500 products. Many are highly industry and theme specific. They can be helpful within their domain but lack compatibility and coherence, and they do not offer viable tools for leadership.

Paul Druckman of IIRC put it best in an e-mail to me on July 26, 2016.

Over the years, I have seen many worthwhile and important initiatives come and go because they haven't gained a broad support base from across the community. [What the markets are] telling us is that they are becoming confused by the alphabet soup of different initiatives and frameworks out there, without a roadmap to know which ones they should be using when. What we urge our friends and partners to do is to become more aligned, to start using consistent language and definitions, so that users can understand how and why they should be evolving their approach to value creation.

What is lacking from these cornerstone efforts? In a word: *measurement*!

The reality is that current initiatives and standards were developed to satisfy external stakeholders, not to manage a business. There are already too many players and standards in the first leg of this SVC journey, but there is still no playing field for progressive companies to compare themselves to or learn from other leaders—which should be encouraged by their boards. They lack both a standard for measuring intangible assets and a clarity in defining the path to value.

The milestones ahead will be a gradual commitment to systemic participation. Though the "value frontiers" will differ by company, they will be bound by a broader vocabulary of material proxies.[6] As we develop this vocabulary, we will make use of currently available sources, and companies will begin to navigate more cohesively in the eyes of all constituencies.

I see this as a new standard for transparency and responsibility that will transform the thinking and behavior of CEOs and boards regarding the role and purpose of corporations in our society. Standards will emerge that steer both corporate missions *and* the collective game of enterprise.

1. We will see a credible job of identifying proxies and linking them to financial performance in a way that is clear and replicable.

2. We will witness more commitment to chosen proxies.

---

6 Proxies that are company-general and specific, policy and disclosure, ratings and rankings, with and without company input, nearly all publicly available.

3. We will see a correlation of these proxies to financial performance within a framework that acknowledges materiality and weighting by industry.

4. We will have access to a standardized framework of these correlated proxies and see companies test their mettle against it, using it in the spirit of coopetition to lift the tide of win-win economics for all.

WE MUST ALL DARE TO LEAD

From here forward, we have to think in terms of interconnectedness and systems. The purpose of a system determines its behaviors and outcomes, and thus I say we must all accept the mounting role of business in society—its responsibilities and its social contract. How we model that system will determine whether we can stay on track.

To Industry Associations

You must own and perpetuate the agenda of SVC and a framework for intercorporate advancement. This can't be done by individual companies and leaders alone. There needs to be collaborative actions by industry associations.

Industry now needs to take ownership of the measurement agenda and develop credible frameworks for integrating environmental, social, and governance factors into the management of business and finance. Companies need a double bottom line measurement system that is based on what factors are driving economic and social value and that measures both. When it comes to finance, however, we have to go further and translate the benefit of the double bottom line into financial value.

To Companies

You must make your purpose statements more strategic and adopt a framework for SVC as soon as possible.

Corporate leaders (and investors) need to see the measurement of sustainable value creation as far more than a reporting requirement. They must see it as fundamental to navigating a changing world.

To CEOs

You must lead toward long-term victory and demonstrate personal character that is in line with your company's stated purpose.

There are codes of ethics and codes of professionalism that should be considered in terms of the individuals in leadership positions rather than just thinking about the corporation as a whole.

To Investors

You must foster more stable, interlinked corporate stances. Be a role model for more considered, less turbulent investment styles.

Win Bischoff suggested in his speech at a Financial Reporting Council symposium on September 20, 2016, that "investors should consider carefully how their behavior affects company behavior and understand how their motivations drive company incentives."

To Board Members

You must challenge your CEOs and fellow board members to find solutions far beyond the short-term and narrow bias of shareholder value.

In his address, Win Bischoff said that "establishing a company's overall purpose is crucial in supporting the values and driving the correct behaviors" and that "boards should give careful thought to how culture is assessed (measured) and reported on. A wide range of potential indicators are available."

To You, Dear Reader

Be an owner. Act like one regardless of your level or job description.

Many of you are now on the front lines of balancing these forces within your professional environments. Others of you are studying to enter the brave new world of commerce I'm describing. Others of you might be in roles that are hardwired to societal goals. Or you might be sensing that your purview allows more (or demands more) than simple compliance with business norms.

KEEP IT SIMPLE

In my world, there is a critical need for a new and simple tool because what gets measured is what matters. Given the importance of long-term intangibles and trust, we need measurements that are linked to a new frame of reference because current decisions are too often made on the basis of a flawed framework that relies almost exclusively on financials, the balance sheet, and a short-term narrow focus on how and what value is being created.

This new paradigm will offer a number of measurements. What's needed is the ability to understand what matters and how those measures interact. We need to recognize that the measure for each vital "capital" (financial, manufactured, human, intellectual, natural, and social) might be different but that they feed off one another over time. This calls for a shift in mindsets as we move from awareness to collaboration and on to some form of shared measurement and, finally, a self-regulating "race" toward success that will lift all ships.

In summary, it demands a stronger call for enlightened corporate leadership, what I call "the license to lead." And this applies equally to directors!

The process of developing this framework will redefine success for tomorrow's companies. It will transform the thinking and practices of present and future CEOs and their boards about the role and purpose of corporations in society as they explore the incentives that drive behavior while creating sustainable value.

Furthermore, the process of establishing the measurement framework of sustainable value creation and embedding purpose and values in it no matter what form the tool eventually takes will be based on these three critical pillars: long-term thinking, trust in business, and the critical role of intangible assets in value creation.

Finally, the process will provide the opportunity to bring leaders together around SVC and inspire a "license to lead" mantra, with model companies serving the needs of shareholders and broader stakeholders by driving business performance and acting as a positive force for society.

WILL YOU TAKE THE BATON?

I have had the privilege of "moving the needle" in building awareness of what must happen as business leadership concentrates on the central themes of long-term thinking that increase the value of intangible assets and foster trust in business. While, at age eighty-seven, I might not have enough time or a platform to drive this kind of leadership and corporate behavior, I do have more than enough time and energy to be a cheerleader for those who do.

Anything we create of substance or meaning in this life relies on choices that are consistent with our deepest values. I firmly believed this as I promoted a major turnaround in business thinking. We are close to changing how global businesses navigate the future in cooperation with the broader opportunities of society. This is my call to action; can you make it yours?

Every business needs a purpose—and a better way to measure their work against the efforts of others.

AFTERWORD

A TIME TO REFLECT

This revisiting of my life's journey has been both educational and refreshing as well as humbling. More than anything, it has served to remind me how grateful I am to so many, especially my family. What started out to be the story of my life, a memoir of sorts to "catalog" the many family stories I seem to be remembering and retelling as I get older, has evolved into an effort to equate these stories and experiences to my inner "purpose," which has taken me down paths of conquest—and some failures (viewed now through my rearview mirror).

You might wonder why I titled this book *Running on Purpose*. First, I did run on purpose: to win Olympic gold, to be the best in my event, to realize my father's 1924 Olympic dream, to distinguish myself—all pretty selfish, I admit. But second, I ran powered on purpose, driven by purpose, and inspired by purpose. You might say that my resilience was born of purpose.

I have pursued many paths in my journey. Outside of a broken leg at age six, I have enjoyed excellent health until the last nine years. In that time I've endured shoulder surgery (I fell off a new bike), two hip replacements, angioplasty, and aortic aneurysm and bladder surgery, all of which reinforce the old adage: Growing old is not for sissies! My involvement in sports, both as a competitor and spectator, has always been very important—even when I coached and played softball on a church-league team that finally won its first game after two years! Golf is such a great, and difficult, sport; you can't imagine my anticipation at becoming an honorary member (after fifty years) of the Pine Valley Golf Club, which has been regularly voted the best in the world!

Travel for business or pleasure is in my blood. I've already gone through several "bucket lists"! I like the planning, execution, and memorializing of my travels. But I'm always very pleased to be home these days in the Endless Mountains of Pennsylvania, where the deer eat all the shrubs and the day lilies in early July smile at you every morning. You can tell from the structure of this book how important friends and family have been to me. I have depended on them. They have inspired my drive. I have been very fortunate to stand on the shoulders of giants. I work at nurturing friends and family, our greatest assets.

Finally, I am excited about our future and our grandchildren's future, which brings me full circle as to why I have written this business memoir. I hope to inspire a much broader

Always ready to run on purpose. Clockwise from upper left: five years old in 1934; at Mercersburg Academy, 1946; the Olympic finals, 1952; with three-year-old granddaughter, 1998; at Cornell, 1951.

audience by telling the story of a boy who left the track but never stopped running and who proudly bore for twenty years the scars and successes of challenging corporate turnarounds. Ultimately, I want this book to be a blueprint for societal change at a pragmatic level that intertwines family, business, and the innovative spark that drives us all. For the reader, I brought together stories, ideas, and strategies that have engaged the titans of industry as well as budding entrepreneurs. Taken together, these stories illustrate what I call the more socially conscious core of business, and I hope to offer solutions for sustainable practices that are so provocative and inspiring that readers will draw on them for generations.

ACKNOWLEDGMENTS

Running on Purpose is a business memoir largely influenced and inspired by many people. It is my first book, and since I've reached the age of eighty-seven, it is likely my last.

This book would not have been possible without the unfailing and creative support of Judith. She has made so many sacrifices in order that I could share my journey with family, colleagues, and strangers.

The inspiration for this story is my father, who was my very best friend, mentor, and "coach" for fifty-four years. We had a unique relationship that was forged out of love and respect, and family is a constant theme in this book. In many ways, the idea of a memoir was born out of my sharing family stories with my children and grandchildren, and they have each gone out of their way to encourage me in the codification of my journey. I am particularly grateful to David and Jim for their exceptional contributions.

In writing this book, I have turned to many people for research, advice, and encouragement. Margaret Coady, my senior partner for eight of my thirteen years at CECP, was an invaluable collaborator in fulfilling our mission, and she contributed significantly to chapter 11. I learned so much from CECP directors and chairpersons, many of whom have generously contributed endorsements of this book; it was a powerful board as we encouraged the rare potential and shared responsibility of some of the world's leading global executives in advancing solutions to the world's greatest challenges. I also want to thank Richard Edelman for writing the foreword. Who better qualified to speak to trust in and the purpose of business?

THOSE WHOSE SHOULDERS
I HAVE STOOD ON

In addition to my family, I could not have done what I did when and how I did without the significant help, love, encouragement, challenging, and mentoring of many others. In many respects, this book, this journey, is a tribute to those who played key roles in my development and successes. And when they learned that I was writing this book, they asked to tell their stories of praise, which you have seen earlier in the book. I am so indebted to great CEOs such as Marc Benioff, Doug Conant, Dan Doctoroff, Paul Druckman, Henrietta Fore, Bob Harrison, Erika Karp, Bill McDermott, Terry McGraw, Barry Melancon, Jim Murren, Marilyn Carlson Nelson, Jean

Rogers, Ed Rust, and Sandy Weill. And such great authors and publishers as Roger Bannister, Ken Blanchard, and David Schner. Such great consultants and teachers as Dominic Barton, Bob Eccles, Doug Hale, Jane Nelson, Chris Pinney, and Gerry Roche. It doesn't get better than that!

The life of a CEO, especially one who is an avowed workaholic, can be lonely, but that is where mentors prove important. And I have been blessed in this regard throughout my life. Starting with my father, I count my coaches at Mercersburg and Cornell, John Nichols at ITW, Susan Murphy at Cornell, and my regents and directors at Mercersburg and CECP as pillars of strength.

Along with the invaluable contributions of my wife, I could not have done this book without my writing collaborator, James Cockerille, who found my voice on the page and is largely responsible for bringing my journey to life with his creative style. He has been a perfect partner, joined by Dan Farley, my "consigliere," and Greg Smith and David Hough, who were responsible for book and cover design and line editing and copyediting, respectively. Finally, I must thank Anna Gratz Cockerille, James's wife, for her lasting support of the process and wisdom as editor and contributor. I am indebted to this great team that I learned so much from.

It has been my intent to give you a front-row seat to my experiences and connect with you on an emotional level through my stories. I share my purpose with the intent of inspiring yours.

ABOUT THE AUTHORS

Charles H. Moore, Jr., is a former businessman, philanthropist, Olympic gold medalist, and renowned champion of societal reform.

Born August 12, 1929, in Coatesville, Pennsylvania, he served as executive director of the Committee Encouraging Corporate Philanthropy from the organization's founding in 1999 until February 2013. *Corporate Responsibility* magazine recognized him as 2008's CEO of the Year for Nonprofits and NGOs and presented him with its Responsible CEO Lifetime Achievement in Philanthropy award in 2013.

He is a 1947 cum laude graduate of Mercersburg Academy and a 1952 graduate of Cornell University. At Mercersburg, he served on the board of regents from 1996 to 2005 and was named the class of 1932's Distinguished Alumnus in 2002. *Cornell* magazine declared him the "3rd greatest athlete ever at Cornell"; he has also been elected as a lifetime member of the Cornell Council.

A large portion of his life was spent with corporate turnarounds, acting as president and/or CEO of a number of multinational manufacturing companies including the Lenape Forge division of G+W, the Lapp and Allied Thermal divisions of Interpace, Clevepak, and Ransburg, as well as serving as managing director of the investment banking firm Peers & Co., CEO of the management consulting firm Peers Management Resources, and vice chairman of the investment advisory firm Advisory Capital Partners.

He also enjoys a unique reputation in track and field, and has been elected to the halls of fame of USA Track & Field, the New York Athletic Club, and International Scholar-Athlete, among others.

As a student at Cornell University, Moore won NCAA titles in the 440-yard flat race in 1949 and the 220-yard hurdles in 1951. He won the indoor IC4A 600-yard run in 1950 and the indoor AAU 600-yard run in 1952, setting meet records in both races. He also won four straight AAU titles in the 400-meter hurdles from 1949 to 1952. Moore was inducted into Cornell University's inaugural Athletics Hall of Fame in 1978, and the Outstanding Senior Varsity Athlete Award at Cornell is named for him. He was also a member of the honorary societies Aleph Samach and Quill & Dagger.

Charlie won a gold medal and set the Olympic record in the 400-meter hurdles in the 1952 Summer Olympics. He finished second in the Sullivan Award balloting for top U.S. amateur athlete in 1952, and was selected as one of 100 Golden Olympians in 1996. Throughout his career, Moore never lost a 400-meter or 440-yard hurdle race.

From 1994 to 1999, he was the director of athletics at Cornell University. Charlie is also a former member of the President's Council on Physical Fitness and Sports and a national board alumni member of the Smithsonian Institution. From 1992 to 2000, he was a public sector director of the United States Olympic Committee and the chairman of that organization's audit committee. He was also the chairman of the USOC's 2012 bid city evaluation task force.

Charlie has served as a director for many for-profit and nonprofit organizations, including Indiana National Bank, Turner Corporation, Sports Authority, Smithsonian Institution, Smithsonian American Art Museum, and the National Art Museum of Sport. He currently serves on the board of GBC Health and on several advisory boards. With a strong interest in governance and a strong commitment to developing the next generation of leaders, he has regularly contributed to codes of business ethics and business conduct.

He remains an active voice in the business and athletics communities, most recently contributing an endorsement for Doug Conant's best seller *TouchPoints: Creating Powerful Leadership Connections in the Smallest of Moments*, as well as writing the foreword for Marc Benioff's *The Business of Changing the World*. Moore received the 2010 MDG Award for Business

Community Leadership from the United Nations and the 1984 Herbert Adams Award for service to American sculpture from the National Sculpture Society.

James Cockerille is an identity consultant with more than twenty years of worldwide experience. Stressing a principles-first approach, he works regularly with executive leaders on issues of integration, organizing for action, and defining the purpose of their organizations. He has held strategy leadership roles with Landor, Interbrand, and most recently as global strategic lead at FutureBrand. James is based in New York City, where he worked with Charles Moore, Jr., to reposition CECP and develop the Institute for Sustainable Value Creation. He holds a BFA with honors in design with a minor in ethics from Carnegie Mellon University.

INDEX

Note: page numbers in *italics* indicate illustrations.

Peers Management Resources, 230

Pembroke College, Oxford, 177

Penn Central, 110

Penn Hall, 67

Penn Relays, 44, 46, 50–51, 163

Penn State, *42*, 45, 46–47, 50–51, 57, 59, 68, 70, 72

Pennsylvania map, *42*

PepsiCo, xiii

Perlman, Joel, 135

Petitions Committee, Cornell, 74

Pew, Arthur, 57

Pfizer, 109, 193

Philadelphia, 165

Phillips Exeter Academy, 64

Picasso, Pablo, 151

Pine Valley Golf Club, 85, 222

Pinney, Chris, 227

Plato, 38

Pollard's Vision (horse), 51

Porter, Michael, 213

positivity, 17, 24–26

Powell, General Colin L., 198

presidential encounters, 178–181

President's Council on Physical Fitness and Sport, 180–181, 231

Prince Andrew, Duke of York, 174

Prince Charles, Prince of Wales, 174

Prince Edward, Earl of Wessex, 174

Prince Philip, Duke of Edinburgh, 34, 161, 173–175

Princeton University, 64, 131, 176

proxies, 215–216

PULSAfeeder, 88, 90, 100, 115

Puritan, The (Saint-Gaudens), 155

purpose, importance of, 208–209

pursuit mindset

action builds buoyancy, 15–17

"can do," siding with, 28

embracing, xvi–xvii

Tenet #1: Get Clear on What's Important, 17–19

Tenet #2: Find the Nearest Path Forward, 19–21

Tenet #3: Shift into Action, 22

Tenet #4: Don't Take No for an Answer, 23–26

Tenet #5: Up the Ante, 26–27

vision, starting with, 13–15

Quakers (Society of Friends), 40, 44, 81

Quill and Dagger, 230

Quito, 83

racehorses, 51

racing. *See* Olympic Games,

measurements, 214–215, 219–220

must-haves for, 210–211

premises, 209

purpose, importance of, 208–209

as purpose of business, 212

readers and, 218

stakeholder concerns and sustainability factors, 211–212

standards, 215–216

system trends driving, 212–213

value, definitions of, 211

Sutherland, Anne (Fuchs), 169

Swedish settlers, 44

Switzerland, 113, 114–115, 119

sword, holding loosely, 26

Sydney, 83

Tampa, 182–183

Tanger, Jack, 66

Tanner, Harold, 130

Target, 172

Teagle Hall, Cornell, 136

Theological Seminary of the Reformed Church, Lancaster, Pennsylvania, 64

thirteen-stride approach, 7–8, 12–13, 37

three iron, 66

Tiananmen Square, 118

Title IX, 127, 132

Today Show, The, 198

Tokyo, 117–118

Toledo, Ohio, 120

Torin Corporation, 100–102, 106, 149–152, 157

Torrington, Connecticut, 100, 149, 150

Touche Ross and Co., 101

TouchPoints: Creating Powerful Leadership Connections in the Smallest of Moments (Conant and Norgaard), 203, 231

Tower Club, New York City, 125

Townsend-Greenspan, 106

Towson, Maryland, 54

track and field. *See also* Olympic Games, Summer 1952, Helsinki; pursuit mindset

4x400-meter relay (1952 Olympics, Helsinki), 32

220-yard hurdles, 230

400-meter hurdles, 3–10, 7, 9, 230–231

440-yard hurdles, 231

440-yard flat race, 230

600-yard run, 230

AAU, 74, 167, 168, 169, 230

"Crip" Moore's running

Virginia Military Institute (VMI), 71

vision, 13–15

Volcker, Paul, 187

Waldorf Astoria, the, 34

Wall Street, xiii, 81, 145, 203–204

Wall Street Journal, the, 148, 170

Ward, Charlie, 94

Ward, John Quincy Adams, 153

Ward Manufacturing, 93

Ware, Barlow, 126

Warner, Jack, 71

Washington, D.C., 119, 121–123, 126, 141, 148, 171, 182–183

Washington National Cathedral, 123, 141

Washington Post, the, 156, 184

Water for South Sudan, 85

Watson, Gene, 90

Wawaset, Pennsylvania, 43–44

Weber Shandwick, 194

website, family, 84

Weill, Sandy, 171, 173, 192–193, 227

West Chester, Pennsylvania, 67

Westchester County, 168

West Hartford, Connecticut, 93

Weston, Josh, 172

White, Stanford, 155

White City Stadium, London, 32–33, 176

Whitehead, John, xii, 170, 172, 187, *187*

White House, 178–181

White Plains, New York, 96, 106

Whitman, Walt, 44

Whitney Museum of American Art, 150

Whittle, Harry, 4

Whole Foods, 172

Wichita, Kansas, 34

Wikipedia, 200

Wilder, Thornton, 172

William E. Simon Track, Cornell, 135

Williams College, 162

Williams Cup, 67, *68*

Wilmington, Delaware, 34

Wilson College, 67

Windsor Castle, 175

Winokur, Pug, 110

Winter Olympic Games, 83

Wolfensohn, Jim, 171

Woodward, Joanne, 170

World Bank, the, 171

World Economic Forum series (Davos), 194

World Series, 163

Wyeth, Andrew, 43, 44

CPSIA information can be obtained
at www.ICGtesting.com
Printed in the USA
LVOW12s2356120218
566362LV00001B/62/P